'A riveting new book ... Connor's spare and clinically crafted reporter's skill masks his anger and enhances the harrowingly drawn-out aftermath of the tragedy, and the illustrious club's shoddily neglectful part in it'   *Guardian*

'Elegantly written and compelling reading' *Yorkshire Post*

'*The Lost Babes* is that rarest of United tomes; one which actually adds another dimension to the club's history rather than providing a simple rehash'   *FourFourTwo*

'There have been countless books about the [Munich Air] disaster, but Connor manages to bring a fresh eye to the topic ... A thorough, and thoroughly moving, piece of work'   *Daily Telegraph*

'Written with consummate skill and no little humour. Highly recommended'   *When Saturday Comes*

'An uncomfortable read, *The Lost Babes* is a genuine effort to provide some context to the lives of those survivors whom the author believes were both victims and forgotten'   *Sunday Business Post*

'Not the first book ab... : one of the best'   *...raph*

'The stories of the survivors make painful and at times heart-rending reading. The Glazer brothers should read this book about Munich and its aftermath. They might understand then how much the very name still means and why emotions are still so raw' *Manchester Evening News*

'A must-read for sports fans. Connor asks the questions that many were afraid to ask' *Evening Echo*

'The survivors' stories show that there is a far darker side to the legacy of Munich for Manchester United'

Daily Mail

THE
LOST BABES

Manchester United and the
Forgotten Victims of Munich

JEFF CONNOR

HarperSport
An Imprint of HarperCollins*Publishers*

First published in hardback in 2006 by
HarperSport
an imprint of HarperCollins*Publishers*
London

First published in paperback in 2007

1

A CIP catalogue record for this book
is available from the British Library

ISBN-13 978-0-00-720808-1
ISBN-10 0-00-720808-1

The HarperCollins website address is
www.harpercollins.co.uk

To the first Manchester United fan I ever met,
Arthur Clive Connor. And to my mother Nancy,
who had to put up with all three of us.

CONTENTS

LIST OF ILLUSTRATIONS

Page 1: The young prince (Popperfoto) Page 2: Roll models (PA/Empics); Happy days (Popperfoto) Page 3: Well turned out (courtesy of Irene Beevers); Birthday Boy (Solo); Pride of Lions (Manchester Evening News) Page 4: Fear of flying (courtesy of Irene Beevers); Playing his cards right (Solo); The inseparables (courtesy of Irene Beevers) Page 5: Four of the best: Dennis Viollet (courtesy of Irene Beevers), Eddie Colman (Manchester Evening News); Mark Jones (Manchester Evening News); Roger Byrne (courtesy of Irene Beevers) Page 6: Strength in depth (PA/Empics); Happy Valley (S&G/Empics/Alpha); King Alfredo (Popperfoto) Page 7: White rose in bloom (Central Press/Getty Images); Beaten but not disgraced (Empics/Topham); Dublin's fair Liam (Central Press/Getty Images) Page 8: The 1957 League Champions (TopFoto); The last goodbye (Getty Images); Last line-up (Popperfoto) Page 9: The aftermath (PA/Empics); The bulletin (Manchester Evening News); The stricken (Getty Images) Page 10: On the road to recovery (Manchester Evening News); Survivor (Manchester Evening News); Grounded (Empics/Topham) Page 11: The return (Getty Images); First gong: (Getty Images); They also serve (Manchester Evening News); Born again (Solo) Page 12: Safe hands (Manchester Evening News); Well saved (Popperfoto) Page 13: Memories (Action Images); Only a rose (PA/Empics); Return to Munich (Empics) Page 14: Flowers of Manchester (PA/Empics); Lest we forget (PA/Empics); Germany remembers (Man Utd via Getty Images) Page 15: Forever young (Popperfoto); Without farewell (Empics) Page 16: Roll of honour (both Empics)

ACKNOWLEDGEMENTS

I am indebted to many people for help with this book, but specific mention must go to: Harry Gregg, Pete Hargreaves, Mrs Laurie Barton, Andrew Blanchflower, Mrs Joy Worth and Roger Byrne Jnr, Paul Greaves, Jack and Irene Beevers, Mrs June Barker, John Doherty, David Sadler, Rino Gambone, Matthew Wilkinson and Brenda Wilson of the Duncan Edwards pub in Dudley, John Webb, Horace Robinson, Pat Forrest, Albert Scanlon, Paul Windridge, Sandy Busby, Christy, Rita and John Whelan, Helen and Rachel Viollet, Gordon Taylor and everyone at the Professional Footballers' Association, the staff at Manchester's Central Library, Jimmy Armfield, Sean Ryan, David Hannigan, David Meek, Tracey Lawson, Steve Cawley, Fausto Gobbi and Torino FC. Some invaluable sources of reference connected with Manchester United wished to protect their anonymity and I have respected that wish.

THE LOST BABES

The research undertaken by Frank Cassidy and Tony Greenbank on the Duncan Edwards and Dudley section of this book was priceless and my undying gratitude goes to both.

Finally, thanks to everyone at HarperCollins for their belief and encouragement. And without Mark Stanton, my agent, this book would never have been completed.

INTRODUCTION

Manchester United plc can be remarkably sensitive about the subject of the Munich air disaster and, in particular, certain events – or maybe we should say lack of events – in the years following the club's blackest day of 6 February 1958. When I first approached the company to ask for access to records and statistics from the Busby Babes' era the first words of the assistant secretary Ken Ramsden in his office at Old Trafford were: 'We will simply not cooperate with anything that will damage the good name of the club.' This before I had even described the content of the proposed book. Mr Ramsden also asked me if I was 'a fan who is trying to be a writer or a writer who is a fan'. When I told him the latter was the case, I had the overwhelming impression that he, and the Manchester United plc, would have preferred to be dealing with the former, of whom there have been many.

I was also informed that I would have to secure permission from the plc's chief executive to talk to employees, past and present, including Mr Ramsden's mother and aunt, who ran the laundry at Old Trafford in the Fifties. But all my e-mails and telephone calls to the then CEO, Peter Kenyon, went unanswered. Someone closely connected with the club also took it upon himself to telephone some potential interviewees in advance to warn them of me, and the subject matter I intended to broach with them. Happily, these pleas fell on deaf, and defiant, ears. It is safe to say, however, that this book was written in spite of Manchester United plc and is unlikely to be found on sale in the Old Trafford Megastore.

Over a period of three years, this book caused much soul-searching about content and motivation. At one stage work on it was halted for over twelve months, mainly because I began to believe that some of the criticisms levelled in these pages – that a number of people had sought to profit from Munich – could justifiably be applied to me. In the end, I chose to agree with a member of one of the Munich families who told me: 'This is a story that should be told.'

Jeff Connor
Edinburgh
February 2006

THE
LOST BABES

1

THE FLOWERS OF MANCHESTER

First of all, a confession. In what amounts to a small lifetime since 19 February 1958, I have only been to one football match at Old Trafford. What is more, I haven't lived in Manchester for almost four decades and in that period have been back to the city on maybe five occasions, and never for any length of time. In many red-tinted eyes this will immediately place me in the same dubious category as Zoe Ball, Eamonn Holmes, Angus Deayton, Simon Le Bon and the millions of other surrogate fans worldwide who have chosen to attach themselves to Manchester United, the 'part-time supporters' reviled in terrace song and on the multitude of websites devoted to the club.

But there's worse: when I did return to Old Trafford as an employee's guest, in October 2002, it was to join Roy Keane's despised corporate spectator brigade in the club's Platinum Lounge where we scoffed, not prawn sandwiches, but paupiette of plaice, stuffed with cockles, and washed down with a bottle of Château Guirauton 2000.

The sixty-or-so current and potential sponsors dining there that night included a smattering of semi-famouses headed by Angus 'Statto' Loughran and Derek 'Deggsy' Hatton and we had been met at the doorway by the Platinum Lounge's extremely famous, and very canny, host ('Don't I know your face?' asked Paddy Crerand of me). Over coffee, a liveried waiter took my order for 'your half-time drink, sir' before someone remembered there was a football match on that night and I retired, in the company of executives from Boots the Chemist, Fuji Films and Ladbrokes the Bookmakers, to my comfy, padded seat in the North Stand to watch Everton dispatched 3–0.

The atmosphere, even when United scored the three goals in quick succession to secure a late victory, was curiously antiseptic, particularly among the support around me. True, clenched fists were occasionally raised self-consciously, but no one once left their seats, even for a goal. The representatives of Fuji Films seemed more concerned with the number of times play went close to their one million pounds a year revolving trackside advertising hoarding than the quality of the football, and the only evidence of real passion came from a large Liverpudlian accompanying Deggsy, whose language was what you would expect from a large Liverpudlian in the company of Deggsy.

The evening's entertainment had cost me £5, the price of a ticket to park my car in a vast, fenced-off area of waste ground on John Gilbert Way close by the stadium, and in the rigidly defined terms of the terraces I plainly do not qualify as a 'supporter', although the current plc may be happy to learn that I have stayed in a nearby hotel part-owned by Manchester United, spent money in the Old Trafford Megastore, eaten three meals in the Red Café and paid two visits, at £5.50 a time, to the club museum. It all depends how you define support.

Before the subscribers to *Red Issue*, *Red News*, *Totally Red* and *Red-whatever-else* start to compile the threatening letters, let me say that despite those forty years spent elsewhere, if people ask me where I am from I always give the answer 'Manchester'. If pressed further I may add (and a northerner's habit of revealing only one item of information at a time has never gone away): 'North Manchester' and, perhaps, 'Harpurhey'. I may also, if I sense a football audience, reveal that Beech Mount nursing home was 100 yards from where Nobby Stiles's father ran a funeral parlour and close by the birthplace of Brian Kidd. If anyone else (and this is always the next question) demands to know where my football allegiances lie I always insist 'United', and if the more erudite look at the evidence of late middle age – grey hair, nascent jowls and alarming waistline – and venture a little further to enquire if I saw the famous Busby Babes in action I can truthfully reply: 'Yes, several times.' They are the reason why the colour red and the place-name Munich represent only one thing to me; why I still feel unreasonably happy when Manchester United win and unreasonably churlish when they lose (even though I feel little or no affinity with the current crop of players, or their manager).

This lifelong and incurable affliction is why, much to the discomfiture and embarrassment of other customers, I wept into my Guinness in a Southampton public house when the man with the flop-over hair lifted that graceless silver trophy at Wembley on a sweaty May night in 1968. And why, as extra-time approached in Barcelona in the Champions' League Final of 1999, I was crouched behind the settee in my Edinburgh flat, out of sight of a taunting television and with a finger in each ear. The Busby Babes are the reason my fealties would have remained unchanged had they won absolutely nothing for the last forty-five years . . . and why, in all that time, I have only once ventured inside Old Trafford for a football match.

On the night of the Everton game, I had foolishly gone along in the hope of catching sight of shades of long ago, imagining that if I half-closed my eyes I would see Duncan Edwards belligerently pushing out his chest and tucking his jersey into his shorts before the game, Roger Byrne imperiously patrolling the touchline, David Pegg tip-toeing down the wing and Tommy Taylor rising to head another goal. But nothing, save a lone banner high in what had once been the Stretford End which read: 'Flowers of Manchester, 1958'. In forty-five years United and Old Trafford had moved on to something I could not recognize and my return ended in a confusion of disappointment, frustration, and something close to guilt.

I have been back for other reasons, most notably on 6 February 2003, when I joined around thirty others under the Munich memorial plaque, in the shadow of Old Trafford's impressive glass façade, to remember the eight players and three officials from the club who had died in Germany at that time, and on that date, forty-five years previously. The plaque, embedded high in a brick wall, is cast in the shape of a football field and lists the lost players: Byrne, Geoff Bent, Eddie Colman, Edwards, Mark Jones, Pegg, Taylor and Liam Whelan, alongside the names of the then club secretary, Walter Crickmer, trainer Tom Curry and coach Bert Whalley, who also perished.

As with so many ceremonial occasions, it was an afternoon replete with symbolism. I had walked down Warwick Road from Old Trafford Metrolink station in the company of a young couple from Singapore, Edmund and Kareen Chan, who were trailing a large suitcase on wheels and had asked for directions to the ground. The Chans proudly informed me that their two five-year-old sons had been christened Ryan and Roy . . . but they, like so many other

United supporters around the world, had studied their history books, knew the story of Munich and understood the justifications for my mission.

At the ground, we wandered around the Megastore, gamely resisting the determined attempts by a lady in a red suit to assign us an MUFC credit card, and then stood in the queue behind a large group of primary school children at a supermarket-style checkout manned by an unsmiling woman with the hard-faced grace of an Albanian customs official: 'You're two pence short,' she snarled at a startled five-year-old girl bearing a tiny fistful of change. In the background, a large man in a shiny black suit, and with the shaven head, gimlet eyes, curly-wurly earpiece and neatly trimmed beard of a nightclub bouncer, kept a twitchy vigil.

Outside, we admired the small collection of wreaths and bouquets on the pavement below the plaque, including a bunch of irises from the Whelan family of Dublin who, via their friend Beryl Townsend in Manchester, commemorate their brother Liam in the same way every year before standing, in the archetypal north-west drizzle, for a minute's silence at the fateful time of 3.04 pm.

The mourners, for that in essence is what we were, were a curiously eclectic bunch: the Chans, a group of five middle-aged men who had plainly taken time off work to remember the heroes of their youth, and youths for whom the only memories of the Busby Babes must have come from books, word of mouth, or flickering newsreel. The five older men stood in a convivial little circle, like veteran soldiers at a reunion, and I thought of approaching them to ask them their memories of 1958.

But I knew what they would say, for I would have offered the same stolid recollections – the time-frozen analogy with the assassination of Kennedy, 'the day Manchester stood still' and the enduring footballing view that 'Edwards was the greatest player I've ever seen'. So I didn't. Instead, I introduced myself to a lone teenager in a United replica tracksuit shivering on the periphery of the gathering. He had skived an hour from the shop on nearby Salford Quays where he worked and was there to represent his father, who was ill and missing his first Munich remembrance day in twenty years. The boy's age, about eighteen, begged the obvious question: no, his father never saw the Busby Babes, but his father's father had. Then, as others around us nodded their approval, he added with a sort of defiant conviction and in the flat, back-of-the-throat vowels of Salford: 'But they were the greatest United team ever, weren't they?'

After the minute's silence, Gez Mason, a well-known United fan and a member of the pressure group Shareholders United, struck up the *Flowers of Manchester*, the song sent anonymously to a local newspaper after the plane crash and later recorded (they wouldn't get away with this now) by the Liverpool folk group, the Spinners. It was as our choirmaster reached the last verse and the words 'Oh, England's finest football team, its record truly great; Its proud success mocked by a cruel turn of fate' that the school children trotted round the corner of the East Stand at the same time as nine smartly dressed businessmen headed in the opposite direction towards the front office and one of the ground's ten conference suites.

The groups passed each other almost precisely where I stood with the Chans. The children clutched their Manchester United plastic bags containing junior tooth-brushes decorated with the logo of Vodafone, Ryan Giggs pencil sets, David Beckham keyrings and Roy Keane posters and stopped and stood still all at once; the suits marched past, hands in pockets, without breaking stride. It was an allegorical moment and a tableau that could be seen as a pertinent illustration of the Manchester United of today: its immutable history, corporate indifference to that history, massive worldwide fanbase, and purposeful beguilement of the very young.

Afterwards, a man about my own age, eyes still wet with tears, shook my hand and thanked me for coming, for all the world like the senior relative at a funeral service. Another complained that there had been no representative of the club, and no wreath from the plc, at the ceremony. I could have explained, but didn't, that by then I had real-ized one thing about Manchester United – and by

Manchester United I mean the faceless grandees located somewhere behind the glass round the corner and not the intangibility that is a football club – and that is that they prefer to confront Munich and its legacy on their own terms.

By 6 pm, when I vacated the Red Café and a plastic chair with the name of Scholes stencilled across its backrest to begin the long walk back up Matt Busby Way to the station, all the bouquets, wreaths and other mementoes had been removed. The mourning, seemingly, had been officially terminated.

Our little ritual had, as always, been mirrored elsewhere. In Belgrade, surviving members of Red Star's 1958 generation, including captain Rajko Mitic and Lazar Tasic, who scored twice in the European Cup quarter-final against United, gathered in the club museum at the Marakana stadium to pay tribute to 'Mancester Junajteda'. Mitic made a moving speech to laud rivals of so long ago, the British Consul was there and a letter was ceremoniously read out from Old Trafford director Sir Bobby Charlton, who could not attend: 'This is indeed a sad day for both our clubs and I very much wished to be with you . . . to remember those who perished on that tragic day forty-five years ago. Unfortunately, circumstances have prevented me from travelling. On behalf of Manchester United Football Club, I send you our very best wishes and our thoughts are with you all.'

On a bitingly cold wet day in Dudley, the Black Country birthplace of Duncan Edwards, fresh flowers had appeared alongside those now withered and faded and a new collection of soaked red-and-white scarves and hats decorated the player's black marble headstone at the town's main cemetery on Stourbridge Road. Similar tributes appeared at the resting-places of the other seven lost players in various parts of Manchester, Salford, Doncaster and Barnsley.

The Whelan family, as always, met by Liam's grave in Glasnevin Cemetery where forty-five years previously over 20,000 Dubliners – including the six-year-old future Taoiseach Bertie Ahern – had gathered to say farewell in an extraordinary outpouring of emotion; and in Munich, close to the site of the tragedy at the village of Kirchtrudering, the trough below the carved wooden figure of Christ had been planted with fresh flowers.

I had also learned by then that, for some, annual remembrance is never enough and that the wounds of loss that have lingered for almost half a century will never heal. June Barker, widow of the genial, warm-hearted centre-half Mark Jones, has been remarried for over thirty years, but says now: 'Mark is buried just down the road from where we live in Barnsley and I can go and see him when I want, which is two or three times a week. On 6 February I am not fit to talk to, so I go with some flowers and just sit there a while. I'm not ever going to forget him.'

In nearby Doncaster, Irene Beevers, the sister of David Pegg, visits her brother at Adwick-le-Street Cemetery every other week. And every other week for the last forty-six years she has found a single, fresh, red flower – usually a rose, sometimes a carnation – in the perforated holder at the base of the grave, placed there by someone with their own reasons to remember a boy who lived, and died, in a different lifetime.

Irene Beevers has never found out who, or why.

2

BLOODY KIDS

Manchester and its battered citizens came blinking back to daylight after May 1945, to find a city, and thousands of lives, altered irrevocably by war. As one of the largest industrialized conurbations in Europe, both Manchester and its twin across the River Irwell, Salford, were inevitable targets for German bombing raids and took a fearful pounding. The onslaught may not have been as prolonged as the London Blitz, but Manchester's teeming terraced ghettoes stretched almost as far as the city centre and the Germans could hardly miss. On the night of Sunday 22 December 1940 alone, German bombers dropped 272 tons of high explosives and over 1,000 incendiary bombs on the two cities over a twenty-four-hour period. There was another, shorter, sortie the following night and in all, the two raids destroyed thirty acres within a mile of Manchester Town Hall, damaged 50,000 houses in the city and erased some of the city's most famous land-marks, including the Free Trade Hall and the Victoria Buildings. Within a one-mile radius of Albert Square and its Town Hall, over thirty-one acres were laid to waste. Salford lost almost half of its 53,000 homes and neighbouring Stretford 12,000.

In Manchester, Salford, Stretford and Stockport combined, the death toll was 596 with 2,320 injured, 719 seriously. Police, fire and Civil Defence services paid the price of their bravery and diligence with sixty-four dead. For many who were uncomprehending children in Manchester at the time, the memories of Christmas, 1940, are not of carols, crackers and paper decorations but of the crump of high explosives, the chatter of ack-ack guns, a skyline lit by flames and the men and women in blue uniforms and tin hats ushering them towards the nearest Anderson shelters or into dank cellars under shattered office buildings.

On 11 March 1941 the Luftwaffe bombers were back, this time with the specific targets of the Port of Manchester and the vast industrial complexes of Trafford Park. Among other contributors to the war effort, this was home to the munitions factory of Vickers and the Ford Motor Company, builders of Rolls Royce engines. The vast silos of Hovis Flour Mill holding grain imported from the United States and the bakery mills of Kemp's and Kelloggs, had also been targeted. All of these stood less than half a mile away from the stands of Manchester United Football

Club on Warwick Road North. It may be fanciful to suppose that one Heinkel 111 was crewed exclusively by Bayern Munich or Borussia Dortmund fans, but the aircraft's bombardier did manage to fulfil the ultimate fantasies of millions of rival supporters then and since, by landing one stick squarely on Old Trafford.

By daylight next day, the stadium, hailed by the *Sporting Chronicle* on its opening in 1910 as 'the most handsomest [sic], the most spacious and unrivalled in the world', was a smouldering ruin. Shrapnel covered the terraces, the turf was badly scorched and the main stand obliterated. It was a wasteland.

Perfunctory attempts were made over the next five years to clear the rubble, employing, in the main, Italian prisoners of war bussed in from an internment camp at Tarporley, in Cheshire, but the sight that greeted the soon-to-be demobbed Company Sergeant Major Matt Busby, of the Ninth Battalion of the King's Liverpool Regiment, when he arrived to take over as the club's first post-war manager on 22 October 1945 was one of forbidding desolation. This was a man who was to demonstrate a mastery of the art of renewal over the next two decades, but this initial labour was one to tax the gods, let alone a thirty-six-year-old retired footballer with little experience of management.

Most historians who set out to chronicle the story of Manchester United manage to compress the period from 1878 to the time of the Scot's arrival at the shattered ground in 1945 into a couple of sentences, such was his impact on the club, and football in general, over the next three decades. But it is worthwhile considering how appallingly mundane Manchester United was prior to the mid-Forties, if only to underpin the popular view that this was truly one of the great football managers, and one who was to create three great sides, of three distinct species, over three different eras.

The two decades before Busby's arrival had been distinguished only by uninterrupted mediocrity – with poor results on the field, low attendances and escalating debt. It was a sequence that reached its nadir in the 1930–31 season when the club, then in the Football League Division Two, went down to six-goal defeats at the hands of Chelsea and Huddersfield. The long-suffering fans, their discontent exacerbated by the fact that local rivals Manchester City were enjoying a period of success, voted with their feet – with fewer than 11,000 watching the 7–4 home defeat to Newcastle United later in the season.

The discontent on the terraces, as it has at every football club since in similar dire situations, became more and more strident. Pressure groups organized the distribution of leaflets outside the ground demanding a new manager, an improved scouting system and new signings. And, as at every football club since, the board ignored all the entreaties and insisted they would go their own way. By the last game of the season, a 4–4 draw with Middlesbrough, most of the support had had enough and only 3,900 were scattered around a stadium that had become a sporting necropolis. In that disastrous season, Manchester United had lost twenty-seven matches, won seven and conceded 115 goals. The board finally decided that enough was enough.

The hapless manager, Herbert Bamlett, a former football league referee who went to work in a bowler hat, was summarily dismissed and secretary Walter Crickmer and chief scout Louis Rocca took over the running of the team. But the damage was almost irreversible and by the end of the 1930–31 season the club was virtually bankrupt. It was clear a miracle, and a miracle worker, was required.

Matt Busby is often cast in the role of the saviour of Old Trafford, the figure who managed to turn brackish water into splendid red wine, but even he would later admit that the recovery was begun, and sustained, by a local businessman, James Gibson. Gibson, who had made his money in refrigeration storage and knitwear, had been introduced to Crickmer by Rocca, the ubiquitous figure who was officially the club's chief talent-spotter, but a man with power and influence at the club, too.

On 21 December 1931, the club secretary, who did not drive, caught a bus out to posh Hale Barns in leafy Cheshire to meet Gibson at his home. The potential benefactor had a

Christmas gift that the incredulous Crickmer could hardly refuse: £2,000 to be placed at the club's disposal immediately and more funds available if the board would reconstitute itself. He would also guarantee the wages of a group of increasingly discontented employees – £8 a week for the first team and fifteen shillings a week for the part-timers and ground staff – and act as guarantor for the club's liabilities. When Crickmer hesitatingly asked what Gibson expected in return for this largesse, the answer was gratifyingly little: he should be elected president and chairman of the new board of directors with immediate effect. Apart from that, nothing, not even repayment of the debt.

Gibson was not, however, the boardroom posturer we have come to associate with so many football clubs, and this shrewd and far-sighted man got to work on the revival of the club at once. He proposed a new issue of 'Patron's Tickets' – an early form of debentures – to raise funds, and although the response to the scheme was lukewarm, it was enough for the new chairman to commit even more of his own funds to the cause. On the playing side, Crickmer and Rocca were able to return to their regular duties when Gibson appointed Scott Duncan as manager and, after escaping relegation in 1933–34, the long climb back to respectability began.

Duncan, a Scot from Dumbarton who wore a carnation in his buttonhole and travelled to work in white spats, seldom left his office, but after a shaky start he proved a canny operator and delegator and the following season, 1934–35, United finished fifth in the league, then put together a nineteen-match unbeaten run at the end of the 1935–36 season to earn promotion back to Division One.

Off the field, Duncan made two of the most significant signings in the club's pre-war history with a classy inside-forward called Stan Pearson joining them in 1936 and a barnstorming, confrontational striker, Jack Rowley, arriving a year later. Pearson, a local boy from Salford, was seventeen when he made his United debut and over the next seventeen years was regarded as the brains of a side that won, under Busby's management, the FA Cup in 1948 and the First Division title in 1952.

Rowley, known as Gunner as much for his service as an anti-tank operator in the South Staffordshire Regiment during the war as his ferocious striking of a leather caseball (a club record thirty-nine goals in that championship-winning season of 1951–52), had slipped through the net of Major Frank Buckley at his home-town club Wolverhampton Wanderers, but made an indelible mark at Old Trafford with a robust and aggressive approach to the game and life in general. Old Trafford apprentices learned to live in fear of Rowley's frequent outbursts and even Busby was to have problems with the player's volatile temperament.

Gibson and Crickmer, meanwhile, had been building bedrock for the club that would sustain it for many years to come. Impressed by the fact that talent such as Pearson's could be found virtually on the doorstep, and for no outlay, they continued to evolve their pre-war brainchild, the Manchester United Junior Athletic Club, to develop youth football. The MUJAC became the forerunner of one of world football's most productive and renowned nurseries.

There were other significant advances that served future managers. Despite debts of over £25,000, United splashed out again by agreeing a tenancy at the Old Broughton Rangers rugby ground close to Manchester racecourse in Higher Broughton, a ground that was later re-christened The Cliff and became the club's famous training head-quarters for the next five decades. Fans, too, benefited from Gibson's diligence and far-sightedness as the chairman lobbied the local Stretford MP to have trains stop on match days at the tiny Old Trafford halt on the London Midland line out of Central Station, and had steps built up from the platform to the ground itself.

Gibson, a man who perhaps deserves a more fitting memorial than the small plaque on the railway bridge above the Old Trafford station, was a shrewd operator. The last year of the war was spent trying to persuade the Government to grant the club finance to redevelop and rebuild the ground after the bombing of 1941 and a licence was finally granted in November 1944. Gibson, who had a number of friends in high places, also managed to spark a debate at the highest level, with a motion put forward in the House of Commons that clubs affected by the war should be granted financial support. Ten clubs, including United, were in need of rebuilding work because of war damage, but it wasn't until three years after Busby's arrival that the club was granted £17,478 to rebuild the ground. The new manager, working in the main from offices in the cold storage plant owned by the chairman at Cornbrook, two miles north of the ground close to Chester Road, could now concentrate on another kind of rebuilding.

When Busby, and his volatile assistant Jimmy Murphy, arrived at Manchester United the club was a microcosm of the city, and Britain as a whole: insolvent, derelict and with a workforce whose best years had been lost to war. The Old Trafford dressing rooms were in a shabby Nissen hut where the south stand once stood and the ground's training area a patch of hard-packed shale behind the Stretford End. Grass grew on the terraces, there were no floodlights and for the next four years home games had to be played at Maine Road, the ground of Manchester City. In those desperate, derelict days this was not the heresy it may seem now as Busby had played for United's cross-town rivals and many of his players had grown up in City-supporting families on the blue side of Manchester. Nor was it an act of charity, City struck a hard bargain, demanding ten per cent of the gate receipts in an agreement signed in June 1941.

The players who came back from the war, arriving in most cases straight from demob, had lost six years of their careers and their footballing skills were in a similar state of decay to their home ground's redundant stands.

Centre-half Allenby Chilton was a case in point. The raw-boned ex-miner had been bought, from Seaham Colliery in Co Durham, as a twenty year old in 1938 and made his debut against Charlton Athletic on 2 September the following year. A day later war was declared. Within a month Chilton had enlisted in the Durham Light Infantry where he served with distinction, twice being wounded in the fighting in France after the Normandy landings. When he arrived back at Old Trafford, he was close to thirty and his best days were over.

The other players Busby was to consider the nucleus of his side – captain Johnny Carey, Pearson, Rowley, Charlie Mitten and Johnny Morris – were all in their mid-to-late-twenties, too, and their service to Old Trafford in the future also had to be looked on as short term. Fortunately for United, every other football club in the country, and every other player, was in a similar state of disrepair. Many post-war careers were to be prolonged by dint of perform-ing on a level playing field.

The post-war team inherited by Busby was reassuringly ordinary; the players were celebrities, but celebrities with the common touch. Many of them were married, lived in terraced houses close to the ground and few had cars.

Gunner Rowley was one of the first on four wheels, buying a four-cylinder, six-seater, Flying Standard – top speed seventy miles an hour – for £300. The wing-halfs John Aston and Henry Cockburn bought a car between them. Chilton and Carey, the captain, travelled by public transport. Carey, like Roger Byrne later, was Busby's on-field alter ego, a figure of quiet authority respected by management and team-mates alike. Strictly Catholic and teetotal, and an astute, moral individual, his obvious leadership qualities led Busby to appoint him captain at a time when some still had reservations about his playing ability. The Dubliner, who had signed for £200 from one of the city's nursery clubs, St James's Gate, in November 1936, was Busby's original all-purpose player. The manager was to become noted for his willingness to try established players in different positions, using the precedents set in his own playing days. Both he and Murphy had resurrected floundering playing careers when switched from their original inside-forward positions, where invariably they had to play with back to ball, to wing-half, where the whole playing field lay in front. Carey was to perform in ten positions for United – including a game in goal – but it was as a calm, assured right-back that he was to make his name. So composed was the United captain that it was said he never got his shorts dirty. Of numerous other beneficiaries of Busby's willingness to experiment, Chilton had been a wing-half originally, full-back John Aston an inside-forward. Bill

Foulkes was a full-back before moving to the centre of defence and Byrne moved from the wing to full-back. Alongside Busby, Chelsea's former head tinkerer Claudio Ranieri appears a model of selectoral consistency.

Carey lived close by Longford Park, bordered by King's Road and Wilbraham Road a mile-and-a-half south of the ground, and an area that was soon a sort of mid-market ghetto for United players and management. The Irishman burned peat in the fireplace of his home at 13 Sark Road, and many of the groundstaff boys at that time can recall earning a few extra shillings for cleaning out the captain's grate, a task, using only a wire brush, which matched the restoration of the Augean stables and which would sometimes take two or three days.

He travelled to work by bus, the other passengers soon becoming immune to the patrician-like figure seated on the top deck puffing away at his pipe. Sightings of Carey and pipe on a bus became commonplace in Manchester and at one time the number of United fans who claimed to have travelled to work with the club captain equated to the several million allegedly at the Eintracht Frankfurt v Real Madrid match at Hampden Park, Glasgow, in 1960, Jim Laker's nineteen-wicket Test at Old Trafford cricket ground in 1956 and England's Wembley World Cup win ten years later.

As a neutral, Carey could have sat out the war when hostilities broke out in 1939 but instead enlisted with the

Queen's Royal Hussars, joining several thousand of his countrymen like the rebel-rousing, folk-singing Clancy brothers, Paddy and Tom, in the fight against a greater enemy. Carey always argued that 'a country that pays me my living is certainly worth fighting for'.

Carey ruled by democracy, leading by example on the field and, off it, prepared to let others have their say. He was well aware that that first great United side contained enough leaders and characters in their own right, notably the gifted England wing Charlie Mitten, Rowley and, in particular, Chilton. Contributions from the captain were often superfluous.

Chilton, the sort of traditional, no-nonsense stopper endemic to every Busby team, and with his square shoulders and centre-parted hair the face of a thousand cigarette cards, did much of the motivational work in the dressing room. In Busby's early days, and after a run of poor form and even poorer results, the manager had gathered his side for a midweek pep-talk. Busby had prepared his speech well, but as he began, Chilton turned to him abruptly and said: 'Just sit down and keep quiet. I'll do the talking. It's our win bonuses on the line here.' Busby did as he was ordered, Chilton spoke, the others listened and the rot was stopped.

Initially at least, the manager had his favourites. He played golf with Carey and Morris, another dangerously outspoken character and a man who at one time considered a career as a professional golfer after a falling out and a subsequent transfer listing by Busby. Busby also relished the skills of Mitten, one of the most gifted wingers of his, or any other, generation but also cursed with an impish and headstrong streak that was to lead to his downfall. Busby adored him, and so did the Old Trafford fans beguiled by his eccentricities and occasional foibles. As the side's leading penalty-taker Mitten would often invite a goalkeeper to point in the direction he wanted him to strike the ball and he would then oblige by sending the ball that way with the goalkeeper powerless. But Mitten was unorthodox off the field too, and after the 1948 FA Cup win accepted a £10,000 signing-on fee and a wage of £60 a week to play alongside Alfredo di Stefano for Santa Fe in Colombia, a country outside the FIFA umbrella. The transaction was carried out in typical Charlie fashion as he not only failed to inform manager or team-mates but also his wife, Betty, who had booked a family holiday in Scarborough. Mitten went to South America, saw out his contract there and came home to find himself suspended. Busby, as he had promised when Mitten first set sail on his South American adventure, unloaded him, at a profit of £20,000, to Fulham.

Busby's first great United side was to provide him with a blueprint for the next, a mixture of cost-nothing locals and former apprentices, alongside one or two shrewd buy-ins, notably the Scot Jimmy Delaney. Delaney, who had won a

Scottish Cup medal with Celtic in 1937, was a fragile-looking wing originally reviled as 'Old Brittle Bones' because of his frequent injuries. It cost Busby £4,000 to persuade Celtic to part with the player in 1946, all but £500 of which he recouped four years later when Delaney went back over the border to Aberdeen: this was the sort of business in which the parsimonious Busby delighted. As for Delaney, he was to have the last laugh on those terrace critics who had questioned his longevity, winning a third winner's medal – seventeen years after his first – with Derry City in the Irish FA Cup Final of 1954.

Delaney was Busby's first outright cash signing and provided him with a tutorial in football management . . . that the occasional shrewd buy mixed with home-grown talent equated to fiscal commonsense.

There were other lessons to be discovered by the young manager, and not just about training regimes and tactics. With so many strong-willed characters, some not much younger than himself, Busby all too often found himself teetering on the line between friendship and the autocracy demanded of a successful administrator. It was a situation he determined never to put himself in again and before long, if players had a grievance they voiced it to Carey, or later Byrne, who would pass it on to the manager. Busby's ability to distance himself from his players when it suited him was to become a hallmark of his long reign. He was also not afraid to unload any potential trouble makers in the ranks, the 'barrack room lawyers' as he called them. Faced with a players' demand for improved bonuses following the 1948 FA Cup Final, Busby met the rebels at the neutral ground of the Kardomah Café just off Piccadilly in the centre of Manchester. After ten minutes of reasoning in that calm, mellifluous brogue, the rebels capitulated. Within twelve months Morris, one of the ringleaders, had been moved on. Many more players of independent mind were to follow him out of the Old Trafford door over the next two decades.

That 1947–48 season proved to be a landmark year for United. Not only did they have permission to begin the work that would eventually enable them to move back to Old Trafford, but the FA Cup win was to be the first major honour under the chairmanship of the indulgent Gibson and the ever-improving stewardship of Busby.

Runners-up in the league for the first two years after the war, the club had also made it to Wembley to face Blackpool in an FA Cup Final still recalled as one of the finest ever. The preparation, however, was far from ideal. Sandy Busby, Matt's son, remembers his father setting off with the team on the Friday night: 'There was no motorway and they arrived at Wembley in the early hours of the morning to play that afternoon. Dad came home on the Sunday in a very emotional mood.'

Despite the rigours of the journey United won 4–2, taking the trophy back to Manchester for the first time since 1909. Gibson, the chairman, suffered a stroke just before the final and could not travel down to London, but the team bus drove straight to Hale Barns on its return to Manchester, and the players presented the trophy to the man whose commitment to the club had kept the football team afloat and had sustained them for nearly two decades. The trophy, in the absence of a suitable glass-fronted cabinet at Old Trafford, was kept in a wardrobe in one of the chairman's spare bedrooms.

On 24 August 1949, United returned home to Old Trafford, established themselves as title contenders for the next two seasons and, finally, in 1951–52, won the Division One championship for the first time in over forty years.

Unfortunately for the club's head architect, James Gibson did not live long enough to add the league championship trophy to the household silverware, as he suffered another, fatal, stroke in September 1951.

As Busby had anticipated, the title-winning season of 1951–52 proved to be the swansong for many of the post-war side and it was plain to the manager that many had long ago stepped on to the downward slope feared by every athlete. When the following season started in alarming fashion with only one win in the first five games Busby acted with decisive ruthlessness.

Albert Scanlon, one of a new wave of young local players recruited by Busby in the early Fifties, says: 'Matt saw the writing on the wall for a lot of the old guard and the kids started coming in. Initially there were no problems. Later there were.'

The emergence of the Busby Babes was not an accident. Busby had assembled a team of scouts, under the control of a sprightly, kindly, former Old Trafford goalkeeper called Joe Armstrong, to scour Britain for talent. Armstrong became a regular fixture at schoolboy and junior games in the north of England in the late Forties and early Fifties while a small team of alter egos – all seemingly similarly small, avuncular and with faces hidden under wide-brimmed hats – performed similar functions in other parts of the country. Most of that talent, as it happened, was waiting on their doorstep and even in the mid-Forties, up to forty, bright-eyed hopefuls from the streets of Salford and Manchester would assemble for weekly trials at Old Trafford. Like many others, Scanlon wonders to this day what became of the hundreds of Billys, Stans, Georges and Harrys who walked down Warwick Road, sandshoes, socks and shorts in carrier bags, to pursue a dream. Most were never seen again, although 'at least they can tell their grandchildren: "I once had a trial for United",' says Scanlon.

Busby's rationale owed as much to a shrewd business brain and his native frugality as a desire to mould a team of willing youngsters in his own image and free of the subversive element represented by players like Mitten and Morris. These young players' future worth to the club could be incalculable, not only in their valued skills on the field but as a valuable asset off it. Busby reasoned that if he could sign ten young professionals on the maximum salary allowed by the League, some £8 a week, it would cost the club £3,500 a year in wages: if only one of the ten made the grade he would be worth between £15–20,000 to the club on the current market values. Good business in any currency. The other nine, if the club did not retain them, would bring back almost as much between them. It all helped defray the cost of rare forays into the transfer market.

Not surprisingly, the ruthless weeding out employed by Busby produced far more failures than successes. It was only the most gifted who survived the pruning.

The recruitment process seldom varied and was typified by United's wooing of David Pegg, a teenage left-winger from Highfields in Doncaster. In South Yorkshire, if a schoolboy was asked what he wanted to do when he grew up the invariable answer was either 'open the batting or bowling for Yorkshire' or 'become a professional footballer'. Most of them finished up following their fathers down the pits. Pegg, who had been spotted as a schoolboy, was one of the few to get away.

When he was old enough to turn professional, on his seventeenth birthday, Busby invited Pegg's father to his office at Old Trafford. Bill Pegg, a miner for forty-eight years, was not the type to have his head turned by fancy promises and with native Yorkshire caution said: 'I want the boy to be happy Mr Busby, but suppose it doesn't go well for him? It's back to the pits. Do you think he will really make the grade?' Busby replied: 'As long as he keeps trying. That's all I ask of any lad.'

Discipline was important, too. 'It's never too early or too late to wear a tie,' Busby scolded the seventeen-year-old Pegg, who had boarded the team bus in an open-necked shirt. They called the senior players 'Mister', knocked on the first-team dressing-room door before entering and this orderliness was maintained in their lives away from Old Trafford, usually in the homes of a series of kindly landladies carefully screened by the club and prepared to report back to Busby on the good behaviour, or otherwise, of their young charges.

Many of them began their new lives in Manchester in the digs of the redoubtable Mrs Watson on Talbot Road close to the county cricket ground and she kept a dozen young players under her roof at any one time. Meals were served around a communal table, some – although not all – helped with the washing up and bedrooms were shared. Mrs Watson had a black-and-white television in the lounge which added to the creature comforts and helped ward off the inevitable effects of homesickness.

The married men lived in club houses, rented for around £3 a week, and most of them within a couple of miles of the ground in the King's Road area.

Housing was one of the few bones of contention in an invariably happy environment. Some wives would pester the club constantly about having a new fireplace built or getting a wall knocked down, the most persistent being Teresa, the wife of Bill Foulkes. A succession of club officials came to dread it when Foulkes would tell them: 'Teresa wants to come and see you.'

Until the age of seventeen, the younger players also went through the motions of pursuing a 'second trade' alongside their playing careers to calm the worries of parents. Bobby Charlton, for example, worked at an engineering firm, Geoff Bent was a trainee joiner, as was Pegg. None of these vocations, it goes without saying, were pursued past the day they signed a full-time contract and became, officially, a Manchester United player.

Busby assembled his backroom staff with equal care. Murphy, the fiery Welshman, was the fulcrum of much of the success of the Busby Babes as we shall see later, but trainer Tom Curry and Bert Whalley, the coach, also played key roles.

Whalley, a former United wing-half who had joined the coaching team after his playing career ended in 1947, was third in command after Busby and Murphy and in many ways appears to have been ahead of his time in terms of the psychology of dealing with young players. A handwritten letter would be delivered to each of them every Friday with a detailed report on how he thought they had played the week before, along with a description of the team they would be playing the following day and detailed insights into the modus operandi of the man they would be marking, or vice versa.

Curry had been a wing-half with Newcastle United for eight years in the Twenties and, like a later generation, lost most of his career to a world war. A product of the South Shields junior sides, he had worked with Newcastle youngsters in the club's North-Eastern League side and his first job as a trainer was with Carlisle United, before he arrived in Manchester in 1934. Along with his 'deputy trainer' Bill Inglis, he wore a white coat to work, both of them resembling rather jolly cricket umpires. While Murphy snapped and snarled, they smiled and cajoled.

'Our whole little world revolved round Jimmy Murphy, Bert Whalley and Tom Curry,' says Scanlon. 'The staff made it so happy, people like the laundry ladies. The older players were more reserved but they would still join in the fun, that was the secret, although it would take nothing for someone like Jack Rowley to snap at you. You had respect for the first teamers, but the kids were really in a little world of our own.'

The Babes' surrogate fathers forgot nothing, according to Busby's son, Sandy: 'Tom Curry, like Bert, was a devout churchgoer and when the team went away, he would go round the lads and find out what religion they were and one of his duties was to go and find out where their nearest church was. He'd get you up in the morning. He'd even get my dad up.'

Along with Whalley, who had been taken on the last trip as a bonus, and Walter Crickmer, who had worked so long and hard with James Gibson to resurrect Manchester United, Curry was to die at Munich.

Tom Jackson, the football writer who covered United for the *Manchester Evening News*, and another Munich victim, is often acknowledged as the author of the title of the Busby Babes, but the credit should really go to a young sub-editor working on the newspaper at the time. Later to become one of journalism's great sports editors, notably with the *Sun*, Frank Nicklin had showed a flair for alliteration even in those days and his headline above a Manchester United match report on 24 November 1951 – the day United gave first-team debuts to eighteen-year-old Jackie Blanchflower and Roger Byrne – was soon almost universally adopted. Busby himself hated the name, but soon found he had to live with it.

Byrne, who was twenty-one at the time, went on to make twenty-three more appearances in the 1951–52 championship-winning side alongside the grizzled veterans of the 1948 Wembley team, and had even scored seven goals in the last six games of the season from the left wing. But two years later the self-contained grammar school boy from Gorton found himself suddenly the head prefect in a classroom of nurslings. United's away match at Huddersfield on 31 October 1953 is often seen as the defining moment in the history of the Babes when seven players under the age of twenty-two, including a versatile defender from Northern Ireland, a clever winger from South Yorkshire and a muscular wing-half from the English Midlands, appeared in the first team in an otherwise undistinguished 0–0 draw.

Busby had begun to break up his first great side and replace it with an even greater one.

The definition of what constitutes a Busby Babe has always been loosely framed. The obituaries of Ray Wood and Johnny Berry, who made their United debuts in the early Fifties, invariably grouped them as Busby Babes, but in fact they were bought in by United, Wood from Darlington and Berry from Birmingham City.

'Tommy Taylor was not a Babe, either,' says John Doherty, a former United inside-forward who was certainly an original Babe. 'You had to be born in Manchester, or reared by the club. Mark Jones was from Yorkshire, but he was a Babe; Jackie Blanchflower was Irish and he was a Babe. Jeff Whitefoot was a Babe and is still one of the youngest to play for United at sixteen. Him, Brian Birch,

Bob Birkett, an outside right who played for England schoolboys, Mark Jones, they were really the first of them, Jackie Blanchflower, then Dave Pegg and me; Foulkesy [Bill Foulkes] the following year.

'Matt and Jimmy were very choosy about who they brought in. I went to United in 1949 as a schoolboy. I was the last person ever signed by the famous Louis Rocca. I was born in Stretford, just behind the Gorsehill Hotel, and then we moved to Rackhouses. They came to my house in Baguley after they had seen me play for Manchester Boys and I was an illegal signing because I hadn't finished school. Jeff Whitefoot was in the office and I joined him there, answering the phone, helping Les Olive with bits and pieces, training in the morning.'

By the end of 1952 the United system that had unearthed so much promising young talent was in danger of over-reaching itself. It was in a state close to overkill. The youngsters were queuing up for places and Busby and Murphy almost buried under an embarrassment of riches. The problem was, where to find them match practice. The Central League, patrolled in the main by gnarled, combative and finesse-free veterans only too happy to give callow youths a kicking they would never forget, was no place for fifteen or sixteen year olds, the reserve team a step too far. But then, the English Football Association came to the rescue.

The FA Youth Cup was the successor to the County Youth Championship, which had been set up at the end of the war as a means of regenerating lost English football talent. The competition, said the FA, would 'give talented school leavers finding it hard to break immediately into senior football the ideal breeding ground for the footballers of the future'. It turned into something more than that for United.

The original competition had entries from some unmatchable, exotic cannon fodder, in particular Huntly and Palmers Biscuit Factory and Walthamstow Avenue, but at the business end most of the managers of the leading clubs recognized the worth of the Youth Cup and entered teams. Unfortunately for them, most of the country's outstanding talent had already been cornered and United were to win the first five finals, played on a home and away basis, by almost embarrassing margins.

If Busby and Murphy found fulfilment in 9–3 aggregate wins over their supposedly main rivals Wolves in 1953 and an 8–2 dismissal of West Ham United over two legs four years later, Crickmer and the Old Trafford bean counters could rejoice, too, as the fans bought into this joyful peek into the club's golden future.

Results like a 23–0 win over Walthamstow in the first season may have equated to a bunch of cruel boys pulling wings off flies, but with up to 25,000 at Old Trafford for the latter stages, the competition could be seen as a success for Manchester United in every possible way. The precocious skills on display were outrageous. The first overhead kick many of us had witnessed by any footballer was delivered by a blond-haired inside-forward in one Youth Cup game at Old Trafford and the daunting thought for most rival team managers was that this lavishly gifted sixteen year old was still two seasons away from a first-team debut. What is more, Bobby Charlton hadn't cost the club of his choice a penny.

Today's fans at Old Trafford speak in awed tones of the youth team of 1992 which contained Ryan Giggs, the two Nevilles, David Beckham, Paul Scholes and Nicky Butt, but supporters of an earlier vintage will happily cite the side of 1952–53 as their equals, if not betters: Clayton, Fulton, Kennedy, Colman, Cope, Edwards, McFarlane, Whelan, Doherty, Lewis, Pegg and Scanlon. All twelve played in the first team and all were sixteen or seventeen years old at the time. 'You tell people that and they just look at you as if you're barmy,' says Doherty.

The Youth Cup certainly helped the learning process and when they did make the next step up Busby's youngsters were ready. Jimmy Armfield, the former Blackpool and England player, and later Leeds manager and enduring media pundit, first saw the nucleus of the Babes when playing for Blackpool Reserves in the old Central League.

He recalls: 'Bobby Charlton, Eddie Colman, David Pegg, Albert Scanlon, Mark Jones and Geoff Bent were all in the team, which shows how good they were at the time.

United were attracting all the best schoolboys, but the thing that stuck most in my mind was the incredible crowd, around 26,000 at Old Trafford. Blackpool had a fair side and we always used to try and win the Central League but there wasn't much chance with that sort of opposition.'

The Babes, according to Armfield, also represented something else. 'It was an exciting time because we were all children of the war and you could feel the country reviving. They seemed to represent that revival with their youth and energy.'

For Albert Scanlon, the Fifties in Manchester and with United were the golden age in every way. There were the joys of a football adolescence on the field and just as many delights off it.

'Old Trafford was like one happy family,' he says. 'Two ladies we called Omo and Daz, who were the mother and aunt of Ken Ramsden, used to do the laundry and the lads used to take all their clothes to them. "Go and tell Tommy Taylor his shirts are ready," they would say.

'Pre-season, the training was running, jumping, and the only ball we saw was a medicine ball. At training we played married men against single men and it was blood and thunder. Some lads wouldn't want to stop, but Bill and Tom had to have their hour dinner.

'Then the fog used to come on to The Cliff off the River

Irwell and all you could see was this white ball. If it got too bad we played silly games, like hide and seek. Tommy Taylor, they could never find him, he was the world champion. No one knew where he was. Someone else once shinned up a flagpole. Another hid under a wheelbarrow. Here I was, little more than a schoolboy, hiding in a training ground lavatory cubicle while some of football's biggest names tried to find me.'

Despite some of the more bizarre training regimes, Whalley, Inglis and Curry seemed to have hit on one essential for a teenager of any era: life had to be fun.

'We were all big snooker players, and there was a table at Davyhulme golf club where we would spend the Fridays before a game,' adds Scanlon. 'We'd see three films a week, getting in free with the little red card of rules the club gave us. That was a passport to anywhere really. Bobby Charlton used to go to the News Theatre on Oxford Road where they showed cartoons.'

The metamorphosis from lark-happy children to serious and dedicated career opportunists on a football field came twice a week, often with a Wednesday fixture in the A team against local amateur sides and, perhaps, a Youth Cup game on a Saturday. The Babes' precocity, however, did not go down too well with some of the other sides around at the time. Manchester United's main rivals for honours in the mid-Fifties were Wolverhampton Wanderers, led by the elegant England captain Billy Wright and Bolton, who were, as now, the Old Trafford bogey team. Everyone feared their line-up of raw-boned Lancastrians with Fred Dibnah accents – 'when tha's finished with him kick him over here' their fearsome full-back Tommy Banks would enjoin his fellow Burnden Park enforcer Roy Hartle – but the disdain for golden youth was everywhere.

'We played Lincoln in a pre-season game and they had a hard case called Dougie Graham at full-back who was in his thirties and on his way down,' recalls Scanlon. 'The ball came down on the edge of the box and as I hit it he hit me and it flew into the top corner and I didn't know this at the time because I'm laid out. They got the sponge at me, the cold water and capsules of smelling salts and Roger Byrne says to him: "It's a friendly and they are young lads." And Dougie says right back: "Until he's twenty-six he shouldn't be in the fucking first team."'

At Old Trafford, too, some of the older players were to rage furiously against the dying of the light, their frustrations exacerbated by increasingly bolder young players who began to show less and less respect for reputation. One incident, late in the 1954 season, was to demonstrate perfectly the growing schism between the United past and its future.

Eddie Lewis, a striker who had been signed as a schoolboy, weighed thirteen-and-a-half stone by the age of seventeen and had scant respect for reputations. Reg Allen, the goalkeeper signed for £12,000 from Queens Park Rangers, was similarly well built. A man who would not go out training until he had his shirt washed and ironed, and his shorts and socks washed, Allen expected respect by right.

Albert Scanlon takes up the story: 'In the first-team dressing room there was a cabinet on the wall and in that cupboard, a bottle of olive oil, a tin of Vaseline and a jar of Brylcreem, all used by various players for hair grooming. The Brylcreem belonged to Reg Allen and Reg had his own ideas about everything, particularly about Reg. The unwritten rule was that you didn't touch anything of his.

'But one day Eddie walks in the first-team dressing room and straight over to the cabinet where he took a dollop of Reg's Brylcreem. "Fuck Reg!" he says. It took three people, me, Bert Whalley and Bill Inglis to get Reg off Eddie, who by then was going blue, with his tongue coming out. Reg looked at his mark again and walked out. Eddie learned his lesson all right, he never made that mistake again, but there were little things like that going on all the time.'

It was clear the old order was on the way out; swaggering youth on its way in. 'Bloody kids' Allen may have christened them, but these bloody kids were perhaps the only young people of any generation, before or since, not to horrify and antagonize their elders. What is more, at an age traditionally one of uncertainty they had already discovered a purpose in life and a means to escape circumstances which, to put it mildly, were far from ideal.

3

NEAREST AND DEAREST

Late in 1959, the researchers for a projected twice-weekly television drama series, based around the characters in a fictional north-west of England street, began to scout locations in and around the cities of Manchester and Salford. In particular, they were looking for a suitable backdrop for the opening credits. These titles, accompanied by a mournful trombone solo and a panned shot of a mangy black cat atop a grimy row of back-to-back terraces would eventually become the most enduring and instantly recognizable in the history of British television. The series makers initially christened the new series *Florizel Street*, but at the suggestion of a cleaning lady at Granada television studios, who thought that name sounded too much like a detergent, later renamed it *Coronation Street*.

The Street, before double glazing, Thai brides, drug abuse, kidnapping and murder arrived forty years later, was all urban banality. It offered a composite of grey, gloomy streets, gossipy neighbours, ghettos of close relatives – but oddly in the baby boomers era no children – and an existence that revolved around the local pub. Most viewers outside the city took it as an accurate portrait of inner-city Manchester.

This world of hairnets, curlers, busty barmaids and ceramic ducks above the fireplace did not find total favour with the city's real-life natives, however, many arguing that few of the characters in the *Street* possessed the traits that defined Mancunians. The actors, as the script demanded, called a spade a spade all right, and all possessed a deliberate and occasional comical manner of speaking. Some combined that odd mixture of thrift and yet generosity endemic to northerners, but *Coronation Street* missed one aspect of Manchester in the Fifties and early Sixties entirely: the sense of unity born out of abject, post-war circumstances. The early *Street* scriptwriters clearly believed that a sense of community equated to pub gossip and affairs with the neighbours. Perhaps they should have examined the real-life model in greater detail.

Archie Street in Ordsall, a few hundred yards from Trafford Wharf and within a mile of Old Trafford football stadium, was the original for those TV credits. *Coronation Street*, then and now, did not own a celebrity, nor a resident of any status – unless we include the philandering factory owner, Mike Baldwin – but Archie Street possessed both in the cheeky and gifted wing-half of the Busby Babes, Eddie Colman, who was born and spent all his brief life there.

Eddie was brought up by his parents, Dick and Liz, at Number 9, later to become the titular home of the *Coronation Street* siren Elsie Tanner, and although Archie Street didn't have a Rover's Return, there was an off licence, a corner shop which sold everything from newspapers to fire lighters and a church, St Clement's, on the other side of Ordsall Park. It was from here that an army of small, well-scrubbed boys and girls set out in procession in the first week of every July through the parish on the traditional Whit Walks. In the afternoon, concerts and cricket and football matches entertained the youngsters and when a leather case-ball came out, the undoubted young star of St Clement's was Eddie Colman.

The Colmans' only child was nine years old when Germany raised the white flag and the bunting and banners came out in Archie Street. In a scene mirrored throughout Britain on that May day in 1945 the women of Ordsall – most of their men were still away in various theatres of war – rooted out their best floral frocks and pinnies for an impromptu knees-up. There were marches and bands and picnics on hastily erected trestle tables and in nearby Monmouth Street a celebratory bonfire was lit using the wooden legs from redundant household chairs. There were Union Jacks everywhere, fluttering alongside the Stars and

Stripes and even the occasional Hammer and Sickle. Portraits of Churchill adorned house windows and V signs were painted on the sooty brick walls of the houses. The dark days were over.

Eddie had been hurried by his parents to a street shelter for much of Christmas 1940 as the Luftwaffe pulverized Salford and its surroundings, the German airmen using the shining length of the River Irwell as a flight path. In the indiscriminate bombing, 9 Archie Street survived intact although just across the Ship Canal incendiaries set ablaze the pavilion and wooden stands of Lancashire County Cricket Club and destroyed Old Trafford Baths on Northumberland Road. One parachute land mine which floated down on to a power station at Trafford Park failed to explode, and was besieged by local children trying to pinch pieces of the silk canopy.

Incredibly, within four days the civil defence and fire services had the 431 major fires in the city under control and Liz Colman's main complaint when the all-clear sounded was about the film of dirt that had infiltrated her well-scrubbed home.

An ordeal like this merely served to reinforce a bond already made strong by the hardships of existence in Salford in the Forties and Fifties. Like every other house in the neighbourhood, 9 Archie Street did not have a bathroom and Eddie washed standing up in the kitchen sink or, on special occasions, his mother would drag the tin bath in from the hook on which it hung outside. The outside toilet was shared and young Eddie soon learned the timing of the subtle cough that would signal occupancy of the shared loo when approaching footsteps were heard on the cobbles outside.

Monday was traditionally wash day, using a tub and mangle – the Servis twin tub, labour saver of a million housewives of the future, was still beyond the family budget of most – and as the family did not possess a refrigerator it meant a daily trip to the shops for a full-time housewife like Liz Colman.

In the manner of Salford, the Colmans' household was cheerfully matriarchal. Dad handed over his pay packet on a Friday night and mum put on one side money for the rent man, electricity and Christmas Club and then tipped him his beer and cigarette money. Eddie would be granted his sixpence a week pocket money. He was educated at Ordsall Council School, where lessons were written out in pencil in longhand atop ancient wooden desks and where a clapper bell summoned children from a dank asphalt yard to lessons. The school can boast three very distinguished old boys in the footballer and, in a later era, Allan Clarke and Graham Nash of the Hollies, one of several Manchester groups who vainly tried to emulate the fame and status of the Beatles in the Sixties. Nash, later to become even more celebrated as the twee songwriter and singer in the supergroup Crosby, Stills and Nash is still remembered in

Ordsall for his performance as an Ugly Sister in the school's version of *Cinderella*.

This, then, was the background and environment which shaped the personae of one of the most dazzling and beguiling of the Busby Babes. Colman's style of play in the school team matched his character and that of the street urchins of Salford: cheeky, extrovert and yet generous (he was to score only two goals in the whole of his United career). He also went in first wicket down for Salford and Lancashire Boys' Cricket team and it would be true to say, as with most of the Busby Babes and young sportsmen of that era, that sport provided an outlet and opportunity that upbringing did not.

Colman's path to Old Trafford followed lines that were to be mirrored in every one of his United contemporaries: kickabouts in the street and impromptu matches on 'red recs' – levelled rubble among the bombsites – that scarred young knees. Then schools football, lads' football, followed finally by a tap on the door from the United scout.

He was the original local boy, in every sense of the words. Archie Street was within walking distance of Old Trafford, half a mile away, and the young player's route to work took him up Trafford Road and over the swing bridge across the Ship Canal at Wharf Way. Often he was late, and Jimmy Murphy soon became immune to Eddie's standard excuse that the bridge, which straddled the main

Manchester and Pomona Docks, had been raised for a passing ship just as he arrived. Murphy, trying his best to look and sound exasperated, would castigate the little wing-half. But always with a smile, for he adored little Eddie.

Eddie's gifts were obvious to Busby and Murphy from the start . . . the famous body swerve that earned him the nickname of Snakehips, the adroit drag-back, the push and run into space and the startling speed off the mark for a boy described by the Northern Ireland goalkeeper Harry Gregg, who joined the club from Doncaster Rovers in December 1957 as 'a wee wag with a beer belly'. And all done with an infectious *joie de vivre*, like a cheeky fifth-former playing truant from school, that captured so many hearts at Old Trafford.

Duncan Edwards, his muscular partner in the middle of the park, was both bigger and more famous then and now, but Colman struck a chord in the hearts of the United support that lasts to this day. He was one of them.

The Colman wiggle could be as disconcerting and baffling to team-mates. 'I remember the first time I played with Eddie and even now it's hard to believe this happened,' adds Gregg. 'I was in goal and Eddie at wing-half and I was a wanderer. If the ball went forward twenty yards, I went forwards twenty yards if it came back twenty I came back twenty. Eddie got the ball and he does this, a wiggle, and I found myself doing the same thing.'

Despite his stature, he was not a soft touch. The fledgling footballer's boyhood hero was Ronnie Allen, the West Bromwich Albion forward who, at 5 ft 9 in, was not only the smallest centre-forward ever to play for England but one of the few English players Eddie could look straight in the eye. In an early encounter at The Hawthorns, Allen fouled him in the clumsy manner of all forwards and Colman, who had learned never to turn the other cheek as a teenager in Ordsall, went after his illustrious opponent. As the two bantamweights squared up, it was United's captain Roger Byrne who stepped in as a mediator, leading the irate wing-half back to his own half.

The fans' love affair with a boy who was to make only eighty-five first-team league appearances had begun long before his first-team debut, aged nineteen, in November 1955. As part of three winning FA Youth Cup sides, one of them as captain, Colman's skills had already become part of pub and terrace folklore before he lined up against United's old *bêtes noires* Bolton at Burnden Park in 1955 for a match in which he was to make an indelible mark and astonish even seasoned campaigners including the opposing captain, Nat Lofthouse. United lost 3–1, but a new star was born and Colman's influence on the side that won the Championship in consecutive seasons, 1955–56 and 1956–57, was immense, with his wickedly incisive passing and devastating dribbling. Busby and Murphy, wisely, made no attempt to stifle the occasional eccentricities.

Nothing, it seemed, could prevent the boy from Salford from making an indelible impression on the game.

If his predecessors at Old Trafford like Carey, Chilton and Rowley had seen their careers and lives disrupted by calls to the armed services, Colman, like every other youngster in Britain between the ages of eighteen and twenty-five, found potential disruption in the National Service, that curse of youth in the Fifties. Originally set at eighteen months, the term of conscription was lengthened to two years in 1950 – much to the dismay of the reluctant conscripts – at about the same time as United's younger players were peering ahead at what they hoped would be great football careers. Instead, the dreaded medical, the ten weeks of basic training, the parade ground, psychopathic sergeant majors and the delights of spit 'n' polish beckoned. Worse, with the outbreak of the Korean War in that year, the unrest in Malaysia and Kenya and the EOKA terrorism campaign in Cyprus, there was a real fear that they could finish up shooting at enemy soldiers rather than the opposition goal.

The reality, however, was gratifyingly different for any servicemen of even average sporting ability and most of them never set foot outside these shores in uniform. Ronnie Cope, who joined the club from junior football in 1951 and could claim to have been one of the original Busby

Babes, was called up in 1953 and expected to be posted abroad, possibly to the army of occupation in Germany.

Cope says: 'I was on my way when an officer came along and pulled me and seven other footballers out of the ranks to start up a football team in the unit. I would play in the Army team during the week, then go home at weekends to represent United. The Army actually got permission from United for me to play. I was paid £1 a week by the Army and the same from United as a retainer plus a match fee. I was never paid the £7 a week of the contract but the club did reimburse the train fare for going back north – if we could provide a receipt.'

Colman, who served in the Royal Signals at Catterick, was also recognized by a senior officer at once, spirited away from the other ranks, and given the duty of physical training instructor combined with an ill-defined role as the camp rat-catcher. Both sinecures gave him ample time, not only to head out to the local pub with his Signals mate Peter Swan for a few beers, but to carry on playing football throughout his two years in uniform.

Others were also wrapped in services cotton wool and in the early Fifties the Army could field a team of awesome international class – and usually did. Jimmy Armfield did his National Service between 1954 and 1956 based at Lancaster, and later Aldershot, and played in a British Army team that included Bill Foulkes, Colman and Edwards. He recalls gleefully: 'To be honest, I can't remember us ever

losing and we had a fixture list that included Glasgow
Rangers and Everton and we even beat Northern Ireland,
who were a very good side at that time. Eddie was a push
and run player, he would shuffle and then go into space. He
was a very buoyant character as well and I can remember
him getting up at the front of the team bus in Germany to
lead a sing-song.'

Back in Civvy Street, or rather Archie Street, the little
Salford extrovert lived life to its fullest. Dick and Liz
Colman proved to be remarkably tolerant and accommo-
dating parents and happily indulged their only son when he
organized several memorable parties. Their neighbours
soon became immune to the sight of most of the
Manchester United first team arriving at the Colmans' tiny
terraced house to drink and dance the night away.

Eddie was also, in his own eyes at least, the club's trend-
setter. While Friday and Saturday-night best for most footballers consisted of ill-fitting jackets and wide trousers with
broad turn-ups, Eddie embraced the latest fashions.

'When I met him he turned up in a duffel coat and a
peaked checked cap on and told me he was the most
forward dresser of the lot,' says Harry Gregg. Later, when
the teddy-boy craze swept Britain, Colman bought a jacket
with a velvet collar and bumper shoes and forsook Sinatra
and Sarah Vaughan for Bill Haley and the early Elvis.

Inevitably, he occasionally came close to overstepping
the mark, at least in the eyes of some of his seniors.

'I remember David Pegg and Eddie and myself got home late one night after a party and we were down at Old Trafford next day,' says Sandy Busby, who socialized with most of his father's young players. 'The state they were in. David and Eddie were trying to stay out of Dad's way, but Dad had a habit of going in the dressing room and going for a pee and usually while he was there he would ask Tom Curry about any injuries from Saturday. He went in the loo on the left of the big bath and came out a couple of minutes later saying: "Tom, tell Pegg and Colman they can come out of the toilets now." They were unshaven and dying. Dad knew where they had been.'

Dad always knew that. Manchester has always been a village posturing as a large city and as many famous footballers have found since, there have always been spies willing to tittle-tattle, with the hypocritical indignation of the frustrated and the plain jealous, to the hierarchy at Old Trafford. The sum of all the Babes' misdemeanours probably added up to one week in the life of George Best, but they still had to watch their p's and q's when out and about in Manchester. Then they discovered girls.

'Back in 1957, we used to dance a foot apart,' Joni Mitchell was to sing much later in a concise summation of courtship of that era when romance was conducted with a space between girl and boy that was not always metaphorical. If they had reason to believe otherwise, most parents would ensure that daughters were home alone by 10.30 pm, that engagements lasted at least twelve months and that permission had to be given in formal fashion by the father of the potential bride.

Girls have been regarded by football managers of every generation as an unnecessary evil. Then, as now, there was no shortage of admirers willing to lead professional footballers off what their clubs would regard as the straight and narrow. By the time of Munich, however, most of the United team was spoken for. Byrne, Bent, Mark Jones, Jackie Blanchflower, Viollet, Gregg and Johnny Berry were married, Liam Whelan and Duncan Edwards engaged. Tommy Taylor and Eddie Colman were 'going steady'. The only one who looked likely to remain a bachelor for the foreseeable future was David Pegg, the winger blessed with the dreamy-eyed, film-star looks and flashing smile, and a boy quite happy to break a few female hearts without the slightest sign of commitment.

The rituals of courtship went ahead in the hundred or so cinemas, dance halls and nightclubs that enlivened Manchester in the Fifties. The city centre had the Gaumont and Odeon cinemas on Oxford Road and the Gaiety on Peter Street where *Gone with the Wind* ran for over a year in front of full houses every night. The Empress in Miles Platting, once the Empress Electric Theatre, was another popular haunt while the Cinephone on Market Street was a slightly more risqué venue, earning a dubious reputation for showing 'foreign' films with titillating titles such as *And God Created Woman* or *L'Amore*. And for the younger, less cerebral, footballers with time on their hands in the afternoon, the masked avenger Zorro and inter-planetary hero Flash Gordon put wrongs to rights in the matinées at the News Theatre on Oxford Road.

Learning to dance properly was a social necessity, too. At the Ritz Ballroom in Whitworth Street aspirant Fred Astaires could hire a professional partner and whirl and twirl in front of a live big band, and there were specialist teachers like Tommy Rogers, who ran a studio on Oxford Road.

'You worked your way up,' says Sandy Busby. 'Going to the Plaza was a big scene. That was on Saturday night. Sunday it would be Chorlton Palais and Levenshulme Palais. There was drink because you needed the Dutch courage to go up and ask a girl for a dance and most of the lads were quite shy. David Pegg was always well groomed, very, very smart. Dave, Tommy and Jackie were always big pals, they used to knock around together. They all had similar backgrounds, all working class, but always very polite, which helped with the girls. If you didn't get a girl you'd go to the Ping Hong restaurant on Oxford Street, across from the old Gaumont picture house. The Kardomah, Espresso Bongo, Deno's, the Continental and the Whisky a Gogo were all popular.

'There was a members' club called the Cromford in Cromford Court, close by the site of the Arndale Shopping Centre, a place where United's players regularly congregated, but you had to behave because Dad would go in there. It was a good place to take girlfriends and as long as they weren't breaking the rules, Dad was quite happy with the lads being there. He'd often send them over a drink. We would go there after the pubs closed to do a little gambling at the tables, watch the floor show, and have a good meal of scampi while it was on.'

The money to feed all this extravagance did go a long way, particularly for footballers who could earn £15 a week, some £9 above the average wage, and the equivalent of around £16,000 a year in modern currency, a sum that would be sniffed at by a Third Division apprentice today. That basic wage could be augmented by a win bonus of £2 and a 'signing-on fee' of £10. The captain Roger Byrne's salary for 1957, for example, comprised a basic wage of £744 from the club, plus league match bonuses of £72, talent money of £45, European Cup bonuses of £60 and an accrued benefit sum of £150. While not actually rolling in the stuff in the manner of his 2005 counterpart Roy Keane, Byrne could be said to have been comfortably off. And unlike many before or since, he had already worked out that he could not play forever, that a footballer's career was far from finite. He had a newspaper column in the *Manchester Evening News*, several minor sponsorships including a Raleigh bicycle endorsement and, in the cerebral manner that always attended his play on the football field, was already, as 1958 and his twenty-ninth birthday approached, planning for a life outside football.

According to Harry Gregg, who can be quite dogmatic about these things, Colman, Roger Byrne, Albert Scanlon, a skinny, but predatory and remarkably consistent inside-forward from Moss Side called Dennis Viollet and the luckless full-back Geoff Bent were the heart of United 'because they were really Manchester Busby Babes'.

At the time of his death, Byrne was long past any definition of Babehood, although he did fulfil the criteria demanded by Gregg. Born in the east Manchester suburb of Gorton, a village of two-up, two-down red-brick Victorian homes brightened only by the 130-acre rural oasis of Debdale Park, Roger was brought up by Bill and Jessie Byrne in a warm, sports-loving family environment. Bill Byrne worked in the furniture department at Lewis's in Piccadilly and his highly intelligent son earned a scholarship to Burnage Grammar School.

Roger played his early football for Ryder Brow Juniors in Gorton and also boxed and played rugby for the RAF, who overlooked the future England full-back for their services football team. His future wife Joy, then Joy Cooper, remembers a 'very good sportsman. It was touch and go whether he played cricket or football, and he was also a good golfer. He also boxed for the RAF, who strangely thought he wasn't good enough for their football team. He was good at every sport, in fact. I loved ice skating and used to go regularly with a crowd from the hospital to the Ice Palace in Manchester. He wasn't supposed to go, but we dragged him along one time. He had never skated before and he just put the boots on and off he went; it really annoyed everyone. We kept saying "for goodness sake, don't fall over" but he never did.'

It was Joe Armstrong who first recognized the promise of the fifteen-year-old schoolboy in a Lancashire Amateur League fixture in 1945. Byrne and a Ryder Brow team-mate, a whippet-thin winger called Brian Statham, were offered amateur forms. Byrne accepted, Statham decided to stick to his first sporting love with happy consequences for both Lancashire cricket and England.

On the football field, Byrne is now acknowledged as one of the Old Trafford greats although, as with so many players, Busby struggled to find the right position for him. His remarkable pace had made him a natural winger initially, but it was a position he despised and it was only when the United management moved him to full-back that he blossomed, as his 275 first-team appearances and thirty-three consecutive England appearances before Munich demonstrate. His calculating football brain, what would be signalled as 'professionalism' today, did not always sit well with rival supporters. 'Booed Byrne Just Loved It' screamed a *Daily Mirror* headline above a match report of a Manchester derby in 1957. Never averse to blatant time-wasting if United were ahead with a few minutes to go, or taking up the cudgels on behalf of more timid team-mates when necessary – he was official minder to Colman and Viollet in their early days – Roger Byrne was barracked at the best grounds in England.

His talent as a full-back was hard to define, although not to the countless players he subdued, including two of the greatest England wingers, Stanley Matthews and Tom Finney. The Wizard of Dribble and the Preston Plumber seldom got much change out of Byrne.

'Roger was very, very bright,' says former team-mate John Doherty. 'He couldn't tackle, had no left foot – even though he played left full-back – was a poor header of the ball, and I have never seen a better left-back in my life. Brains and pace. Tackling was demeaning to Roger. He preferred to pinch it or make them give it him. Jimmy Murphy used to say to the full-backs: "Don't tackle them and they will finish up giving you the ball. You have done your job once they cross the ball." Roger was brilliant at that.'

As a member of the 1951–52 title-winning side, Byrne also retained a certain hauteur, with the gravitas and occasional intolerance of an older generation.

On one pre-season training camp, he cuffed a youth-team player called Wilf McGuinness round the ear for daring to take his chair by the hotel pool, and more than once other Jack-the-lads at United suffered fearsomely memorable bollockings, Eddie Colman in particular. They would never dare answer back.

'Saturday night, we would go out dancing and have a few drinks,' says Sandy Busby. 'Sunday morning it was always Mass with Dad and then I used to go back home and then shoot off down to the ground. All the lads used to go down, particularly if you were injured. There would be a five-a-side or runs round the ground. This Sunday we had been to a party, the usual gang of Eddie, Peggy and myself. It was two or three o'clock and Eddie was there at the ground looking like death and who walks down the tunnel but Roger? He comes up to us and says: "Sandy, would you mind leaving us?" I carry on, Roger walks back up the tunnel and Eddie comes back very red and flustered. "All right?" I asked. "Roger just told me if I don't get a grip, I'll be out of here," says Eddie.'

It was this respect engendered in others, along with a high moral code and a peerless football brain that convinces Sandy Busby to this day that the captain could have succeeded his father and managed Manchester United.

He says: 'I used to see both of them talking quietly together and I was sure Dad was grooming Roger to take over,' he says. Byrne was never a yes man however, confronting Busby on several occasions over the rights of players, their entitlement to bonuses and even on-field tactics. He fell out with the manager at the end of his debut season in 1951–52 over a demand for an increase in bonuses and on another occasion narrowly avoiding being thrown out of the club altogether.

According to the manager's son, 'In his early days Roger was a handful, an awkward bugger. He didn't like playing at outside left, he wasn't happy at all and at one time even asked for a transfer.

'On the end-of-season tour of America in 1952 things got even worse. United played against a team of kickers from Mexico and Dad tells them, "These fellas will try and get you riled but just ignore it, walk away." In the first five minutes Roger gets kicked up in the air and he whacks the next one who comes near him. Off he goes. At half-time Dad walks in the dressing room and tells him: "You'd better get changed. What did I tell you?" Roger was still a bit cocky so Dad says: "Get your gear together, you're going back home." That night Johnny Carey goes to my Dad's room and tells him Roger is distraught. He's in tears. Dad told Carey that Roger would have to stand up at a team meeting next day and apologize to his team-mates and then he can stay. He did. After that, Roger became more of a team man and then he became captain.'

Gregg insists: 'Roger Byrne, who I played against at international level, I thought was aloof until I got to know him. Some people are leaders and he was a great captain and had no fear of Matt Busby. I don't mean fear like a schoolboy and headmaster but in the short time I knew Roger I found he asked the questions and also answered the players' questions. The finest pointer to that was in Belgrade on the last night. The banquet went on too long and at 12 midnight Roger wrote something on a piece of paper which was passed all the way up to Matt. He had written "You promised the lads they could go out after the do. Can we go out now?" Matt nodded his head. That was Roger Byrne.'

Sandy Busby may have been convinced that Roger Byrne would one day succeed his father, but the United captain was already looking in other directions. He had met his future wife when both were studying physiotherapy, Byrne's chosen career post-football. Joy Cooper went to school in Audenshaw, and as a teenager an uncle had taken her to Maine Road to see United, so did know a little about football pre-Roger.

'We met as students,' says Joy who is now remarried to James Worth, a former schoolteacher. 'There was an intake of students and we knew one of them played football. None of us knew any names at United and City and we looked at all these chaps and thought: "Which one is it?" And we couldn't work it out. Roger was only studying part-time and it was going to take him six years to qualify, as he only attended in the afternoons after training in the morning.

'By the time I went to Salford in 1951 a lot of rebuilding had gone on in the town and it was becoming more affluent and a good place to live. We were able to go out more and more. At the hospital ball I went with my girlfriend who was meeting another man and he brought Roger along, so we made up a foursome. We went out and that was it. I soon finished up going to the United home matches and the local away matches, usually with Roger's best man, John Pickles. The wives were treated as any other supporter. After the game I waited till Roger came out to the car park.'

Although many, Matt Busby and his wife Jean included, were convinced that courtship and marriage had doused many of the fires in Roger Byrne, Joy is unwilling to claim any of the credit. 'Matt Busby always told me he was very short-tempered before he became captain, very fiery to begin with and Jean Busby said it was me that quietened him down. We were only married six months so I can't claim any credit for that; I think it was more a matter of giving him the responsibility and him becoming responsible.'

Even after they were married, the young bride found that football was never far away. The ceremony was at St Mary's Church, in Droylsden in June 1957, and a honeymoon was planned for Jersey. Most of the United team, as it turned out, were there and Roger played football and cricket the whole fortnight.

'Jean and Jackie Blanchflower had been married the weekend before us and they were there on honeymoon, so it was the same for Jean,' says Joy. 'We met Peter McParland there [the Aston Villa player who knocked Ray Wood out in the 1957 FA Cup Final] and Jackie and Roger got on like a house on fire with him. Jean and I were not too happy, it must be said.'

Football, and Roger's ancillary earnings that included his lively and well-read column in the *Manchester Evening News*, did afford the couple some luxuries. Their club house was in upmarket Urmston and they also bought a Morris Minor – 'like hen's teeth in those days', according to Joy – to get to and from work, the car happily tootling along at a top speed of sixty-five miles an hour and rocketing from zero to sixty in twenty-four seconds. Once, a year before Munich, it tootled in the wrong direction on an icy Wilbraham Road and careered on to a local resident's front lawn. The occupiers, Matt and Jean Busby, woke to find the club captain and his wrecked car in their front garden, a famous piece of Manchester United folklore.

When Roger died at Munich, two days before his twenty-ninth birthday, Joy had been waiting at home with news of another cause for celebration – she had fallen pregnant and their first child was on the way. A boy, later christened Roger, was born in Cottage Hospital, Urmston, thirty-eight weeks after the crash.

Most of the memories of his father have come second hand from his mother and grandparents, along with old newspaper clippings and a fine and detailed biography by Iain McCartney, but Roger Jnr can also see film of the captain of the Busby Babes in action for Manchester United whenever he chooses.

Footage of that side is extremely rare, but Joy had the original film of the 1957 Cup Final defeat against Aston Villa which features as its centre-piece the Villa winger McParland's X-certificate assault on the United goalkeeper Wood, Blanchflower's heroics as a replacement, and the three goals. She sent it to the North West Film Archive who restored it and sent the Byrnes a tape in return.

On a modern video with freeze-frame it is possible to capture a telling moment shortly after McParland's charge on Wood. Duncan Edwards, characteristically hitching up his shorts as he did as a prelude to any battle, is seen looking down on the prostrate Villa player, and plainly considering reprisal. It is Roger Byrne, arms spread wide, who urges calm. The rabble-rouser of the early Fifties had plainly mellowed and matured into a special leader of men.

Within twelve months, United, England, a young mother-to-be and a distraught north of England mother and father had been robbed of a man Harry Gregg is happy to describe as 'the nicest fellow who ever walked God's earth'.

Jessie and Bill Byrne's grieving went on long after Munich, but according to Joy, the arrival of a grandson helped them cope.

'Dad had great difficulty, although Mum was very strong,' says Joy. 'But she was bitter about fate. There was no blame to anyone, it was just that she had lost her son, her only son. Dad never did get over it. He took it extremely badly. One thing that pulled us all through was Roger, that was one thing to live for and that made a hell of a difference to all of us. We were married six months, and in all I knew him two-and-a-half years. It's not a long time, is it? I don't have millions of memories, but those I do have are very good.'

The bachelor Babes inevitably had more problems filling the time between training than the married men like Byrne. When the fare offered by cinemas, cafés and snooker tables of Manchester had been exhausted, one afternoon venue which earned brief popularity, particularly on a Sunday, was Ringway Airport, south of the city on the edge of the Cheshire countryside. There, a septuagenarian waitress called Amy had taken a particular shine to the young footballers, particularly Duncan Edwards.

He seemed fascinated by flying and between sips of dande-
lion and burdock and bites of toasted crumpet 'the big lad',
as Amy called him, would watch the planes outside take on
board their passengers, taxi out to the single runway and
then head upwards into the grey Manchester sky.

4

A SMALL FIELD IN GERMANY

For the majority of the Busby Babes, the first trip abroad, and their first flight, was to an international youth tournament in Zurich in May 1954. The party was led by Busby and Murphy, supported by Bert Whalley and Arthur Powell, a groundsman who was also a qualified St John's Ambulanceman. Among the fifteen players were Edwards, Charlton, Pegg, Scanlon, Colman and Whelan. This was the nucleus of the effervescent young team who had won the FA Youth Cup for the first of five times the previous season.

Zurich was a voyage of discovery in many ways. The players had to cope with the logistics of applying for a passport for the first time, packing a suitcase to cope with the demands of a week away from home and attempt to cope with the Swiss currency. Busby had also, with a nod towards his chain-smoking staff, Powell and Murphy, warned of the penalties of attempting to bring too many packets of duty-free cigarettes back through Customs, and the perils of foreign foods.

The departure point was Ringway Airport, the forerunner of Manchester International, and named after the road close by the original site in Wythenshawe. Ringway had been opened in 1938, but it was not until 1952 that the airport began twenty-four-hour operations and by 1954 it was handling over 163,000 passengers annually. Air travel, however, remained a massive adventure outside the compass of many . . . and far from the magic carpet ride it is today.

The departure lounge at Ringway was adorned with vases on the window ledges and chairs with Lloydloom plastic backs and sides and, until passengers passed through the door marked Departures and stepped on to the runway tarmac, it was also exclusively all-smoking. Three civilians working in shifts manned the radar station and the method of communication between control tower and incoming and outgoing aircraft was by hand-held telephones.

On board, travellers were cosseted by bilingual air stewardesses (two languages at least were the main qualification before female airline staff were forced to look, and dress, like uniformed Barbie dolls) and in those pre-hijack days food was dished up with silver service. Inside the cabin, most aircraft used on commercial flights featured a collapsible mid-cabin table with chairs facing both fore and aft, a boon to families with children. Later, these tables were to prove just as useful to Manchester United and its enduring, and highly competitive, card school, of which Harry Gregg was the acknowledged Amarillo Slim.

The flight to any city in Europe took little longer than it does today, because in skies almost free of traffic there was no necessity to climb to altitude. The flightpaths to Europe were seldom above 5,000 feet and cabins were not pressurized. The journey gave United's young travellers the opportunity to learn the realities of this new form of travel – that some were good fliers but others chronically bad.

Scanlon, Pegg and Colman revelled in the great adventure while Edwards, despite his schoolboyish fascination with the concept on his day trips to Ringway, found the experience terrifying. Like his captain Byrne, another notoriously bad traveller, he was well aware of the high-profile problems with the Comets of the British Overseas Aircraft Corporation which had culminated in a series of fatal crashes in 1953–54 and resulted in the loss of 111 lives in all. Much nearer home, and just eleven months before Munich, a BEA Viscount Discovery had demolished a row of houses on Shadow Moss Road in Wythenshawe on its approach to Ringway, with all twenty-seven passengers killed. These disasters, coming in the early days of commercial flights, did nothing to allay the players' fears that this was a form of transportation to be tolerated, and occasionally feared, rather than enjoyed.

Paying customers, too, plainly needed unqualified faith in pilots and groundstaff.

That first airborne adventure, however, went without a hitch and United's week in Switzerland proved a resounding success. They began the tournament in less than convincing fashion with a 0–0 draw against FC Young Fellows, a Zurich club side, but decisive wins over Bern and Red Star earned them the silverware in resounding fashion. The Yugoslavs, in particular, simply could not handle the seventeen-year-old Edwards who had made his first-team debut twelve months earlier and who, within a year, would become a fully fledged England international. The brawny teenager, with hapless opponents bouncing off him like small-arms fire off a tank, helped himself to a hat-trick. Boys against a man-boy.

Two more victories in friendlies followed and on the flight home Busby could reflect that Edwards and his teammates had made their mark on Europe for the first time and justified the expense of taking them there. The trip also confirmed his view that English football had to lose its parochialism and expand its boundaries if it was to progress. But Busby was to find opposition almost every step of the way.

The English game at the time was defined by a native insularity that came in many forms. At its most harmless level, many players, administrators and fans genuinely believed that Europeans could not handle the physicality

on which the English game had been built and which characterized the First Division of that time; nor could they
head the ball. The cissies, so we all believed, began at
Calais.

At a more extreme level, the then Secretary of the
Football League Alan Hardaker once told the English journalist Brian Glanville: 'I don't like Europe. Too many wops
and dagoes!' This clueless and self-serving xenophobe, the
worst sort of Lancastrian with intolerance masquerading
as blunt commonsense, was to maintain these opinions
with damaging effect on English football for many years,
until the powers of the Football League were diluted and
Hardaker himself unseated.

There had been earlier warnings that English football
was not as omnipotent as he and other administrators
believed, notably in a shameful defeat by the United States
in the 1950 World Cup finals in Brazil and, more explicitly
and closer to home, in two momentous thrashings, home
and away, by Hungary in 1953.

England and the other home countries had not deemed
the pre-war World Cups worthy of their participation,
maintaining their splendid isolation from football outside
the British Isles. That 1–0 defeat by a team of American
part-timers in Belo Horizonte in England's first World Cup
was regarded simply as an aberration, compounded by the
effects of travel, foreign food and referees who simply did
not know the rules. The BBC did not deem the event

worthy of coverage and only eight English journalists were present.

There were some prophets in this lost land, however. Walter Winterbottom, the national manager of the time, was one who saw the future at once: 'We were so insular that we wouldn't believe that other methods could be used for doing other things, other ways of playing the game could be better than ours, and that had to change, of course.'

It took many years to effect that change.

At the beginning of November 1953, three weeks before the first friendly against Hungary, the world governing body FIFA sent a scratch team of different nationalities to Wembley to celebrate the English Football Association's ninetieth anniversary. A last-minute penalty earned England a 4–4 draw, but observers were impressed by the technical merit of individuals such as Giampiero Boniperti of Italy and Ladislav Kubala, a Hungarian refugee. On 25 November, Kubala's compatriots arrived at Wembley to make up the numbers in a friendly that would surely extend England's record of never having been beaten there by a side outside the British Isles. The fact that Hungary were unbeaten for three years and had won Olympic gold in 1952 seems to have passed the English football cognoscenti by. The country that invented the glorious game, after all, could boast the composed Alf Ramsey at full-back, the bustling Stan Mortensen at centre-forward and the Wizard of Dribble, Stanley Matthews, on the wing. As for Hungary, as one England player chortled to his mates in the dressing room before the game: 'Lads, you won't believe this, they've got a wee fat man playing for them!'

The wee fat man, who turned out to be a Hungarian army major called Ferenc Puskas, was to have the last laugh.

Every team in England at that time lined up the same way: goalkeeper, two full-backs who seldom strayed past halfway, one attacking wing-half and one defensive wing-half sandwiching a centre-half who spent all of the ninety minutes locked in a muscular battle with the opposing number nine. Up front, two conventional wingers supplied the crosses for a centre-forward adept at heading the ball – and not much else – with two inside-forwards alongside him, one slightly deeper than the other.

Hungary played a different game and the startled England centre-half, Luton's Syd Owen, was to put it rather well later: 'It was like playing people from outer space.'

Nandor Hidegkuti had a number nine on his back all right, but the two strikers were Puskas and Sandor Kocsis and the nominal centre-forward spent most of his time in midfield alongside Josef Boszik. The wingers constantly switched stations, adding to the English confusion. The full-backs occasionally overlapped while the forwards often tackled back to help their defence. This was revolution on a grand scale. England simply could not cope and the final score of 6–3 accurately reflected the humiliation. Overnight, Puskas and his team-mates became the Magical

Magyars and none of that magic had dimmed by the following May, when England went to Budapest for the return game. This time they lost 7–1, the heaviest defeat in the nation's history. The lesson of Wembley had plainly not been learned and as the under-employed Hungarian goalkeeper Gyula Grosics was to say later: 'I feel that the English were very reluctant to give up a tradition of a game which was actually their invention and which had brought them so much success.'

The lessons offered by the Hungarians were absorbed in some corners of Britain, however. That first game at Wembley had found some interested observers in Manchester. 'We had gone round to Mrs Watson's where a lot of the lads lived in digs,' recalls Albert Scanlon. 'It was a large house on Talbot Road opposite the bowling green and she had a telly. We didn't have one at our house and I had gone round to watch the Hungarians and I got there just in time for half-time. I remember the score coming up and the commentator saying: "England 2 . . ." whereupon Mark Jones whipped his pipe out of his mouth and shouted "Give it to them, lads!" before the rest of the score ". . . Hungary 4" and it all went dead quiet.'

Busby, too, had watched on television the Hungarians annihilate the pride of English football and had had his imagination fired; he had seen the future.

Others had seen it first. The United manager is often given credit for his pioneering work in Europe, but United were not the first British club to embrace the concept of competition there. Before the first European Cup, in 1956, Wolverhampton Wanderers, United's major domestic competitor in the mid-to-late Fifties, had floodlights at their home ground of Molineux, and had played friendlies against Honved, the Hungarian side, and Dinamo Moscow.

The inspiration for the European Cup proper came from the French sports newspaper *L'Equipe* and its writer Gabriel Hanot, a former French international. His idea of a knockout competition played home and away and featuring the continent's champion sides reached tangible form when eighteen of those teams met in a Paris hotel in 1955 to agree a format. It was a second notable sporting coup for *L'Equipe* which had been instrumental in promoting the first Tour de France fifty-three years earlier.

That first European Cup of 1955–56 proved to be an instant success. There was no English side in that competition but there was a Scottish one – Hibernian and the Famous Five of Gordon Smith, Lawrie Reilly, Eddie Turnbull, Willie Ormond and Bobby Johnstone – who surpassed all expectations by reaching the semi-final where they were beaten by the French side Reims, one of the great unheralded feats of British football.

Hibs were Britain's unchallenged pioneers of long-distance football. The chairman, Harry Swan, had taken the club on tours of Sweden, Belgium, Austria, Germany and France just after the war and in 1953, the Scottish side embarked on a mind-boggling trek to Brazil, taking twenty-six hours to fly from Edinburgh to Rio de Janeiro via London, Paris, Lisbon, Dakar, Recife and finally Rio. There, they stepped straight off the plane to draw 2–2 with the Brazilian champions Vasco da Gama in the Maracana Stadium.

Hibs had maintained long-standing links with Manchester United. Busby had played for the Scottish side before the war and in 1952 took his English champions north to meet their Scottish counterparts in a testimonial for Smith, losing 7–3 at Easter Road. Far from sweeping away English parochialism, the Hibs example went dismally unheeded. The champions of 1954–55, Chelsea, had been invited to compete alongside the Scots in the inaugural championship, but had been browbeaten into refusal by Hardaker, who insisted that the domestic programme would be disrupted by fixture congestion. Chelsea capitulated without a murmur.

Hardaker was to have far more opposition from Busby and his erudite and single-minded chairman Harold Hardman as the Babes, in two seasons of football rich in wit and energy, swept all before them in England to establish themselves as worthy challengers to the best in Europe.

It all came so easily for them. In 1955–56 they had mopped up the championship with two games remaining and with a margin of eleven points over perennial rivals Blackpool and Wolves. Most pundits had wrongly judged that the very rawness of the side – an average age of twenty-two – would mitigate against them, but as Albert Scanlon says: 'We soon made them eat their words.'

Old Trafford became a theatre of broken dreams for opposition sides and the team remained unbeaten at home all season. Colman made his debut that season and with Edwards established as an elemental force in the other wing-half position, United proved unstoppable.

The following season they simply carried on where they had left off with ten wins in their opening twelve games. A blond, ridiculously talented inside-forward called Bobby Charlton began his legendary first-team career in October 1956, putting two goals past, appropriately enough, Charlton. The firepower that Busby could muster was almost frightening. Tommy Taylor, Charlton and Viollet were prolific enough, but the marksman of the season was Liam Whelan, the wraith-like inside-forward who finished with twenty-six goals out of a team total of 103.

United again wrapped up their championship with three games to spare and although they were robbed of a first Double when Aston Villa beat them controversially at Wembley in May 1957, it was apparent that only something extraordinary could prevent them from dominating the domestic game for the next decade. Then Europe beckoned.

Hardaker and the Football League had put pressure on United at the end of the 1956 season, demanding that they ignore UEFA's invitation to compete in the second European Cup tournament, but Busby and Hardman were made of sterner stuff than Chelsea, recognizing not only that broader challenges were needed for the club but also the financial benefits of competing in Europe. They took the decision that was to change the history of the club forever. Hardaker was to have his revenge after Munich, coercing the Football Association to stop United from competing in the 1958–59 competition after they had generously been invited to take part by UEFA. This, rather than the rather dull competition he invented, the Football League Cup, serves as Hardaker's memorial in the eyes of United fans with long memories.

Busby's team made an auspicious but ultimately misleading start in Europe in September 1956, beating the Belgian champions Anderlecht 2–0 in Brussels and then brightening a dreary wet night at Maine Road by cantering through the second leg 10–0 with four goals from Viollet, a hat-trick by Taylor, two goals from Whelan and one from Berry. Try as they might, United could not manufacture a goal for Pegg, the only forward who failed to score. But the urgency and vigour they brought to that first home game in Europe was exemplified by the sight of Colman, his side ten unanswered goals ahead and with the referee ready to blow for full-time, sprinting twenty yards to take a quick throw-in.

Those twelve goals, United's first two-legged win in Europe and this sudden expansion of football horizons, caught the imagination of the country and a crowd of over 75,000 packed Maine Road for the second-round, first-leg match against Borussia Dortmund. The Germans proved far more formidable than Anderlecht, pulling back a three-goal deficit to 3–2 in Manchester and ensuring that it would be Mark Jones and the unsung United defence who would do most of the work in the 0–0 draw in Dortmund.

Then came Bilbao in the quarter-final and an eerie portent of what was to come. United were drawn away in the first leg on a pitch turned into a swamp by continuous rain and snow, but although they trailed 3–0 at half-time they showed indomitable fighting spirit to pin Atletico back to 3–2. The Spaniards scored two more before Liam Whelan took a hand with a much-celebrated solo goal, the Irishman wandering through a paralysed Spanish defence as if in slow motion for forty yards and then lifting a right-foot shot out of the mud into the top left-hand corner. A 5–3 deficit was precarious, but not insurmountable given the potency of a United forward line supported by the voracious Edwards.

There was also a stark glimpse into the future on the return trip home. It had been snowing for twenty-four hours and the team's Dakota, with every hangar on the airfield occupied by benighted aircraft, was left out on the runway with the inevitable result. Mindful that United had to return home for a league game against Sheffield Wednesday on the Saturday and knowing, too, how the

The young prince: Duncan Edwards celebrated his selection for England Under-23s in the way he knew best – with some extra training. He was 17 at the time.

ABOVE: Roll models: Duncan Edwards, Johnny Berry, Dennis Viollet, Bill Foulkes, Roger Byrne, Wilf McGuinness, Mark Jones and Liam Whelan ahead of the sixth round FA Cup tie against Bournemouth and Boscombe Utd, February 1957.

BELOW: Happy days: The 1956 League Championship triumph was marked by a civic reception at Manchester Town Hall. Captain Roger Byrne keeps a firm grip on the trophy.

Well turned out: in public, the dashing David Pegg would always appear immaculately well-groomed.

Birthday Boy: Liam Whelan, on his 21st, blows out the candles, helped by his mammy Elizabeth.

Pride of Lions: Matt Busby with his two England icons, Roger Byrne and Duncan Edwards, in 1957.

Fear of flying: Many of the United players hated it; others, like Mark Jones, Eddie Colman and David Pegg, could tolerate it, on their increasingly frequent flights to Europe.

Playing his cards right: Tommy Taylor at home with fiancée Norma Curtis.

The inseparables: Bobby Charlton, David Pegg and Tommy Taylor spent much of their spare time together, often travelling over to Pegg's home in Doncaster in three identical Vauxhall Victors.

Four of the best: In their own different ways, and in their own different positions, Dennis Viollet, Eddie Colman, Mark Jones and Roger Byrne were priceless to the United cause.

Strength in depth: An unusual team line-up in April 1957: left to right, Ray Wood, Duncan Edwards, Tommy Taylor, Liam Whelan, Geoff Bent, Bill Foulkes, Jackie Blanchflower, Ronnie Cope, Dennis Viollet, Eddie Colman and Johnny Berry.

Happy Valley: United's leading marksman Tommy Taylor forces the ball past Charlton goalkeeper Willie Duff, and defenders Don Townsend and Trevor Edwards, for the opening goal in the league match at The Valley in February, 1957.

King Alfredo: Exiled Argentinean Alfredo di Stefano – here challenging Ray Wood as Duncan Edwards, Roger Byrne and Jackie Blanchflower look on – masterminded a 3–1 home win against United in the European Cup semi-final first leg in April, 1957.

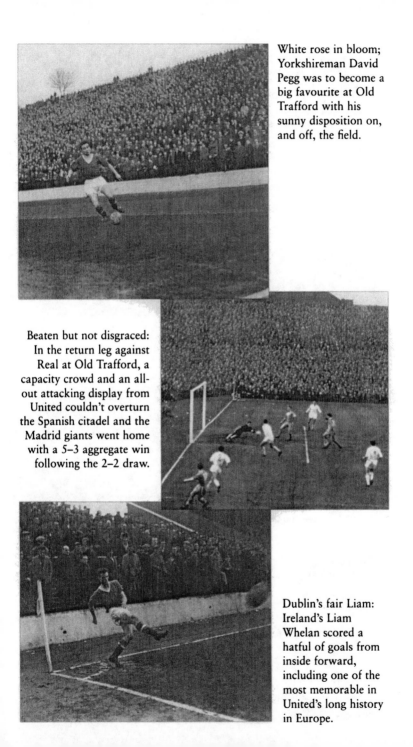

White rose in bloom; Yorkshireman David Pegg was to become a big favourite at Old Trafford with his sunny disposition on, and off, the field.

Beaten but not disgraced: In the return leg against Real at Old Trafford, a capacity crowd and an all-out attacking display from United couldn't overturn the Spanish citadel and the Madrid giants went home with a 5–3 aggregate win following the 2–2 draw.

Dublin's fair Liam: Ireland's Liam Whelan scored a hatful of goals from inside forward, including one of the most memorable in United's long history in Europe.

The 1957 League Champions: United finished with 103 goals and eight points ahead of second-placed Tottenham. Busby defied the Football League and entered his Babes into the fledgling European Cup the following season.

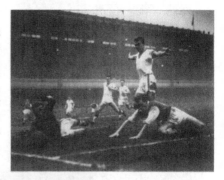

The last goodbye: Harry Gregg saves, Duncan Edwards rides shotgun, Roger Byrne and Bill Foulkes look on as United bid farewell to British football in an unforgettable game against Arsenal at Highbury on 1 February, 1958. Six days later, the dream died.

Last line-up: The famous picture taken in the Marakana Stadium, Belgrade, on 5 February, 1958. Left to right: Edwards, Colman, Jones, Morgans, Charlton, Viollet, Taylor, Foulkes, Gregg, Scanlon and Byrne.

League management committee had viewed their entry into Europe the players, officials, pressmen and airport staff mucked in to clear the snow and ice off the wings. A famous photograph, taken by Liam Whelan, captured the grinning players sweeping away with their bare hands.

At Maine Road in the return leg goals from Viollet, Tommy Taylor and Johnny Berry gave United a 6–5 aggregate victory and a semi-final date with the team who were to prove their nemesis for many years in Europe. Real Madrid, the holders, with Alfredo Di Stefano, Raymond Kopa and Gento in their side, inevitably proved too strong. A 3–1 win in Madrid, and a 2–2 draw in Manchester – this time at the newly-floodlit Old Trafford – took the Spaniards through to a second successive final.

United's first European adventure was over, but they were by no means disgraced. Busby knew he had time on his side and could point out that the average age of his side was twenty-two and that in some areas against them Real had struggled, most notably in their attempts to curb his Schwarzenegger-like centre-forward, Taylor. It was felt that, given time, Manchester United could be a match for anyone.

The last domestic season of the Busby Babes began well, with victories over Leicester at Filbert Street, then Everton and Manchester City at Old Trafford, twenty-two goals coming in the opening six games. United's perennial bugbear, Bolton Wanderers, beat them 4–0 at Burnden Park in front of a crowd of 48,003, but by Christmas United were hard on the heels of the Division One leaders Wolves.

They also made steady, if occasionally shaky, progress on two other fronts. In the FA Cup, a 3–1 win at Workington – a tough proposition in those days, strange as it may seem now – and a 2–0 victory over Ipswich at Old Trafford took them through to the fifth round, where they were to meet Sheffield Wednesday.

In Europe, Liam Whelan masterminded a 6–0 victory over the amateurs Shamrock Rovers in his home town of Dublin; while Dukla Prague were beaten 3–1 on aggregate, but again with a reminder of the perils and difficulties of air travel in the return.

The home leg against the Czechs was almost effortless and, encouraged by a capacity crowd who had bought into the great European adventure, United won with goals from a young Welsh reservist, Colin Webster and the Yorkshire duo of Taylor and Pegg. The away tie proved more hazardous in more ways than one with a 1–0 defeat in Czechoslovakia presaging another scare at Prague airport on the way home.

Fog in Manchester had delayed their flight and with heavy bookings elsewhere there was a real risk that United would miss Saturday's fixture against Birmingham – and incur the wrath of the vengeful Hardaker. It was time to improvise and eventually the players were found places on a flight to Amsterdam after which they took a boat from the Hook of Holland, a train to London and another to Manchester. The large press party followed via Zurich and Birmingham. Tired but relieved, Crickmer and Busby arrived back at Old Trafford determined that the club would not be subjected to the vagaries of commercial flights again; in future they would charter their own aircraft.

United would face another East European army side, Red Star Belgrade, in the quarter-final of the competition that was already beginning to obsess the thoughts of players and management at Old Trafford. The first leg was scheduled for 14 January in Manchester and the return on 5 February in Belgrade. The Red Star match-up would fall between league fixtures against Bolton and Arsenal and the FA Cup tie against Ipswich. It was a taxing schedule, but it was also becoming plain that this side was maturing fast into something extraordinary. Edwards, the insatiable workhorse, had once played four games in a week for United and England, and they appeared physically capable of anything asked of them. Many good judges believed they were capable of a glittering and unprecedented treble, forty-one years before Sir Alex Ferguson's side achieved that feat. They stayed on course in Europe when a goal from Charlton and a rare strike from Colman gave United the edge in a 2–1 first leg victory against Red Star. Bolton were brutalized 7–2, leaving United six points adrift of Wolves at the top of the table and with the trip to Arsenal to come before the flight to Belgrade.

The man on the record turntable at Highbury had played Buddy Holly's chart-topping song *That'll Be the Day* over the tannoy just before the Busby Babes ran out for their final match on British soil. 'That'll be the day when you say goodbye . . . that'll be the day when I die.' The music died twelve months later in an Iowa cornfield; the football five days later on a Munich airstrip. Holly's song, it transpired, was a valediction for both.

The Babes, almost as if sensing that this was their final bow and an opportunity to leave an indelible impression on the game, duly signed off with a triumphant statement of everything that the team stood for. There was dash and enthusiasm that produced five goals and careless youthful frailty that caused them to concede four, Edwards, unusually, being the main culprit.

Over 63,000 were at Highbury for United's first, and last, visit of the season, and they were to witness not only the champions at their best, but also to see Arsenal almost match them. It was an archetypal United performance with Colman and Edwards joining in with the attackers to make six or even seven forwards and the opposition taking advantage of the gaps left in defence. United were first on the score sheet after ten minutes, as Viollet then in his pomp as one of United's greatest-ever strikers, dribbled through the home defence before finding the eighteen-year-old Welshman Kenny Morgans, who had been brought in for Johnny Berry. Morgans' cut-back found Edwards, and he finished off.

This, however, was Albert Scanlon's finest hour and a half. On one of those rare days that any athlete comes to recognize at once, the winger could do little wrong and his direct running down the left embarrassed Arsenal all afternoon. His sprint and cross gave Charlton the chance to finish cleanly and ten minutes later the little Mancunian was away again to deliver another of his dangerous low crosses. Again Morgans supported and Charlton was there again to give United a 3–0 interval lead. It was breathless stuff, and the home side headed for the dressing rooms in a state of shock.

'It was stunning,' said the Arsenal centre-forward David Herd, who was later to enjoy a distinguished Indian summer to his career at Old Trafford in the Sixties. 'I hadn't seen an English side that could do the things they did. I mean, we were all attacking teams in those days; raiding wingers, two potential strikers and a midfield that tended to pour forward. That's the way we played. But United did it all at a different pace. In a way, I was almost enjoying it.' United's bravura display did leave one man unmoved, however. Roger Byrne, with Busby and Murphy for once standing silent, laid into his troops. 'This game is not over,' warned the perfectionist captain. 'We are far too careless at the back. Too lackadaisical.' As so often, he was to be proven right.

Arsenal made some positional changes at half-time with wing Vic Groves swapping positions with the inside-forward Derek Tapscott and the results were immediate.

A goal from Herd and two from fellow forward Jimmy Bloomfield in as many minutes brought the scores level. Back came United. Scanlon and Charlton set up a chance for Viollet, who made it 4–3 and then Tommy Taylor, demonstrating that he was far more than a mere header of the ball, waltzed along the byline before beating goal-keeper Jack Kelsey from an almost impossible angle. Tapscott caused a few flutters among the United support with Arsenal's fourth fourteen minutes from time, but Byrne and his defence held out.

Busby didn't know whether to laugh or cry at the end. But he recognized at once that this team were not going to change their modus operandi, nor would he encourage them to do so. Their foibles had to be tolerated alongside their flair. It was their way and, as if to underline this, a reserve side containing nine internationals lost 6–5 at Barnsley on the same afternoon, giving the former Barnsley player Tommy Taylor some extra bragging rights to go with his goal at Highbury.

Wolves had beaten Leicester 5–1 so United remained third in the league. When Billy Wright and Wolves arrived at Old Trafford the following Saturday it was plainly for a match that could decide the championship. Through to the fifth round of the FA Cup and in the last eight in Europe again, and still viable contenders for a third successive title – a feat only achieved previously by Arsenal and Huddersfield – Busby was convinced now that his side was on the threshold of greatness.

'I felt I was in a position where I could have sat back for ten years while they played, they were that good,' he said.

As he had promised following the near-fiasco in Prague, the club secretary Walter Crickmer had raided the United kitty to charter their own plane for the round trip to Belgrade. With the vital Wolves match looming and the weather forecast for Eastern Europe far from encouraging they could take no chances and British European Airways duly supplied a forty-seven seat Airspeed Ambassador of the Elizabethan class for the sole use of the United party. On Monday 3 February, the team, management and accompanying press boarded G-ALZU under the command of Captain James Thain at Ringway airport for flight B-line 609 to Belgrade via Munich, a non-stop flight being beyond the range of the Ambassador. The Red Star match was scheduled for Wednesday, and the return flight the following morning, Thursday 6 February. Three nights were to be spent in the Yugoslav capital.

The Belgrade match mirrored almost exactly their farewell performance at Highbury and although two goals from Charlton and one from Viollet put United 5–1 ahead on aggregate, the lead dissolved after half-time. Kostic gave Red Star a dream start to the second half with a goal two minutes in, Bill Foulkes conceded a penalty and then Kostic brought the overall score back to 5–4 directly from a free-kick. This had been given away by the European debutant Harry Gregg when the Irish goalkeeper carried the ball out of the penalty area.

From then on it was down to Byrne, Jones and his unsung and overworked defence and they held. United were through to the semi-finals again.

The celebrations went on long into the night. At the official banquet the Yorkshire trio of Jones, Taylor and Pegg gave a rousing rendition of their national anthem *On Ilkley Moor Baht 'At* before, as midnight approached, Byrne showed his strength of character by demanding of Busby that the players be released to enjoy the Belgrade nightlife. Some, in the main the married ones, headed straight back to the hotel, while the bachelors found their way to a nightclub called The Crystal where the merry-making went on in time-honoured fashion.

'I will never forget those young faces, so happy that night when they sang so gaily,' a Yugoslav journalist called Vinko Sale was to recall later. In The Crystal Tommy Taylor and his new pal Dragoslav Sekuralac, who had been ruthlessly subdued by Duncan Edwards in both legs, drunkenly embraced and vowed to stay in touch. Taylor would one day return to Belgrade and the young Yugoslav striker was welcome in Barnsley where the Yorkshireman promised him 'a reet good time'. Later, Sekuralac was to break down and weep when he realized it would never come to pass.

It had snowed virtually throughout the match in Belgrade, but Busby's fervent hope was that the weather would have cleared following the stay overnight. The weather did abate slightly on the Thursday morning when a hungover party re-embarked, but worsened again en route to Munich. By the time G-ALZU landed in the Bavarian capital, it was snowing heavily.

Kenneth Rayment, the co-pilot, produced a bravura piece of flying to bring the Ambassador swooping out of the gloom to touch down at Reim airport amid great plumes of slushy spray and within a few minutes the passengers had disembarked. Boys being boys, Colman and Pegg good-naturedly pelted the ground crew with snowballs and the last hour was spent mainly in the duty-free shop. Pegg, as he always had, searched out a present for his sisters, Liam Whelan a gift for his mum, and the others enjoyed a warm drink before finally, at nineteen minutes past three local time, the flight was called.

On board the Elizabethan, Rayment, who in a minor breach of BEA regulations was at the controls instead of

Thain on the wrong side of the cockpit, requested permission to taxi to the runway and eleven minutes later the Ambassador began its first takeoff attempt. After forty seconds, with the throttle open on full power, both pilots heard an uneven engine note and takeoff was abandoned at once. The plane, like a motor car caught in the first snows of an English winter, slewed under heavy braking in the runway slush and ice. A second attempt was made almost immediately with the same outcome and, with their passengers becoming increasingly worried, the two pilots decided to return to the stand to consult with the ground-crew technicians. Thain's voice came over the intercom in the best matter-of-fact tones of pilots everywhere to announce that due to a 'slight engine fault' he was returning to the apron for an engine check.

'It is hoped it will not be a long delay,' he added. The plane returned to the terminal, where everyone disembarked. The wisecracks and snowball fights had stopped now as the young footballers trudged back to the departure lounge and when the flight was called again, after what seemed to be only a few minutes, some had started to voice their concern. 'We started to think right then that maybe we wouldn't be going home that afternoon,' says Albert Scanlon.

As the twin engines fired and the plane nosed down the runway for its third takeoff attempt, the aircraft's Radio Officer Bill Rodgers made his final transmission to the control tower. British European Airways Flight 609 Zulu Uniform was rolling, he said.

The players had whiled away the first leg of the journey, from Belgrade to Munich, with the traditional games of either hearts or poker, but they were in no mood for that now. The school halfway down the aircraft, comprising Bill Foulkes, Kenny Morgans, David Pegg and Scanlon put their cards away and strapped themselves in. Opposite them sat Ray Wood, Jackie Blanchflower, Roger Byrne, Liam Whelan and Dennis Viollet. Busby and Bert Whalley were just behind the Foulkes group and Mark Jones, Tommy Taylor, Duncan Edwards and Eddie Colman at the back with most of the pressmen. Suddenly, as the plane began to taxi out for the third attempt, Pegg decisively unstrapped himself, stood up and moved to the rear of the plane.

Gregg, who had been sprawled across three seats on his own, noticed how quiet the cabin had become, and glanced across at Byrne, the captain, in search of reassurance. Byrne was white-faced with anxiety. Someone gave a nervous laugh, and Johnny Berry cried out: 'I don't know what you are laughing at, we're all going to be killed' and then they were speeding down the runway, past the point where they had stopped the previous two times, on and on and on. Up ahead on the flight deck, Thain glanced at the airspeed indicator which registered 105 knots.

'When it reached 117 knots I called out "V1" [velocity one, the speed at which it is no longer safe to abandon take-off],' Thain told the official inquiry later. 'Suddenly the needle dropped back to 112, and then 105. Ken shouted, "Christ, we can't make it," and I looked up from the instruments to see a lot of snow and a house and a tree, right in the path of the aircraft.'

As the plane careered off the end of the runway and the noise of swish and slush gave way to a grinding, murderous, scraping, both Scanlon and Gregg heard, from just across the aisle, a voice that would live with them forever: 'If this is death I am ready for it,' said Liam Whelan. Then there was silence.

It was four minutes past four local time, four minutes past three in Manchester.

5

DUBLIN'S FAIR LIAM

If Liam Whelan's faith had prepared a boy of twenty-two for the end, it also helped his family through the black days ahead. A non-smoker, non-drinker, and almost certainly a virgin, the young Dubliner went to Mass every day and most of his acquaintances during his five years in Manchester, players apart, were Catholic priests. Bobby Charlton, who shared a room with his team-mate at Mrs Watson's lodging house on Talbot Road, remembers vividly the Irishman's nightly rituals with his hand-crafted rosaries. The whole life, in so many ways, was informed by preparations for death.

Liam's last words have proven to be an enduring comfort for the Whelan family. His brother Christy and sister Rita were at home with their mother in St Attracta Road, Cabra, on Dublin's northside when they heard that the United plane had crashed. Christy says: 'We heard the gate opening and Charlie Jackson, a great friend of Liam's, was there. Mammy was out in the back ironing. She stood with her back to the sideboard and the minute she saw Charlie she knew something was wrong. But she said: "I know they are home. It's three o'clock, they must be home." And Charlie said: "I am afraid not, Mrs Whelan."

'He had come to offer condolences and finished up breaking the news, although it wasn't until seven or eight hours later that we learned the worst.'

Like many others in Cabra and like many of the families of the players, the Whelans did not have a phone and the club, once the names of the dead had been confirmed, first contacted a neighbour in St Attracta Road.

The caller, and the man who had taken on the gruesome responsibility, was Jimmy Murphy, the Babes' surrogate father and the man who had cajoled, harangued, inspired and occasionally indulged them through their brief apprenticeships.

Murphy had turned up to work late on Thursday having travelled back from Cardiff where the Welsh national side, of which he was part-time manager, had won a World Cup qualifying game against Israel to reach the finals later that year in Sweden. He was walking jauntily down the Old Trafford corridor to his office, whistling loudly as usual, when Alma George, Busby's secretary, stopped him.

'She told me twice,' Murphy was to say later. 'It still didn't sink in, then she started to cry. She said many people had been killed, she didn't know how many, but the players had died, some of the players. I couldn't believe it. The words seemed to ring in my head. Alma left me and I went into my office. My head was in a state of confusion and I started to cry myself.'

But Murphy pulled himself together and, seated in his office in the chilled surroundings of the empty football stadium and with only a bottle of whisky for company, the little Welshman found the relevant telephone numbers one by one.

'The call came to our next-door neighbours at around 11 pm,' says Christy Whelan. 'Mr Murphy told Mammy: "Mrs Whelan, I am sorry, but I have bad news, Liam didn't make it. From all that's left at Old Trafford" – that's how he said it, "from all that's left at Old Trafford – we wish you all condolences and we will be in touch."

'Then there was a knock on the door and the police were there with the news, too. Mammy was upstairs in the bedroom by then and she was still refusing to believe it. When I went up she said to me: "Christy, if he was definitely dead, the police would have to come." And I said: "Mammy, they were here, the police."

'It was one terrible long week before we got him home,' says Rita. 'John Giles came up with his father and some of the other young Irish lads, Jackie Mooney, Jimmy Sheils came over. At the graveside, Mammy was very strong and she didn't weep. It was only back in the car that she cried for the first time and back home the doctor gave her a sleeping tablet. The funeral, at Glasnevin, it was as if the president of Ireland had died. They were thronged from the airport and all the way from Santry and outside Liam's old school, St Peters, all the little children were waiting there; you couldn't get near the church. It was so hard to believe he was only twenty-two and his life had come to an end.

'The worst time was when summer came and we were expecting him home. He had been here two weeks before the crash. He had had flu and Mammy was not too well, either. So he bought her a rose and that was the last thing he ever gave her.'

Whelan had asked to be excused from the ill-fated Belgrade trip. He had just lost his place in the team to Charlton, was suffering with a heavy cold and felt he could benefit from a rest in Dublin. But Busby told him that 'it wouldn't look right' if he didn't travel with the squad. Despite this, the Whelans never did question the perversities of fate, or indulge in some of the recriminations that later were to characterize many of the players who survived.

'We accepted that he had gone to heaven and that God had wanted him,' says Rita. 'We never asked why. On the fortieth anniversary we were listening to Harry Gregg's version of it, but we never went into things like that. Liam died on the Thursday and the following morning, the first Friday, was Communion and Mammy had us round Christ the King Church in Cabra. It was our faith brought us through it. Nor have we ever asked anything of United. All the money in the world couldn't bring Liam back to us.'

Liam's father, John Whelan, had died in 1942, eleven years before his son signed for Manchester United and the family – two other brothers, John and Christy and sisters Rita, Maura and Alice – were ushered into adulthood by their mother Elizabeth. Rita lives in the family house in the tight, working-class community of Cabra today.

At Christy's home in Portmarnock, Co Dublin, tea is served from beneath a Manchester United tea cosy and reminders of their lost brother are everywhere. There is a peace and serenity about the house, something you can only define as a goodness and these qualities are reflected in the family Liam left behind. There is little doubt, either, that these qualities were inherited from Elizabeth Whelan.

Christy says: 'Daddy worked for the Dublin corporation, and contracted TB. Mammy was left with all the children and we never wanted for anything. None of us were working and although we didn't have everything, we never wanted. Even football boots. Cabra was a great area, all working class. We played football on the road and in the playground and actually preferred that to going to the pictures. We had a team in the playground called the Red

Rockets, and this team went unbeaten for two years. Mum worked for the council looking after nurses going off to England or America and she had to leave at seven in the evening, getting back at three in the morning and she would cycle through the blackout.'

Liam's first club was Home Farm, still one of the most fertile breeding grounds for Irish football talent, and one that at various times has boasted Johnny Carey, Liam and another great Whelan, the former Liverpool player Ronnie. The great United and Leeds player John Giles and the Leeds full-back Gary Kelly, along with some fifty senior Republic of Ireland internationals, also began their careers there. It was Liam who persuaded Ronnie Whelan's father, Ronnie senior, along to the club. Ronnie Whelan senior's grandchildren and Liam Whelan's nephews wear the light blue of the club, now known as Dublin City, today.

Home Farm has always taken as much pride in its players' attitudes off the field as in their achievements on it. In the early days, many of the team were altar boys from Corpus Christi Church, and it was this institution, his close family ties, and his beliefs that shaped the young life of Liam Whelan. Those, and his unmatchable footballing talents. He found his stage in Manchester, but his heart remained in Ireland.

Christy remembers: 'Liam went to United in 1953 and he would come home for the internationals. The local kids would knock on the door: "Is Liam coming out to play?"

He'd go out in the street to play and come back later and say: "Well, a hat-trick at Dalymount and a hat-trick on the road, what do you think of that?"

'He was always very humble and very down to earth. And he loved his family. In Manchester he got very homesick and never really settled down. "I wish it was all over so I could come home and open a business," he would say. But he did find a home there. He had lived in digs at Mrs Watson's, then left to go to Mrs Gibbs, but he suffered terrible homesickness. Sean Dolan, who worked for Louis Edwards, who later became the Manchester United chairman, lived on the edge of Stockport and Liam was there one day playing with the two children when all of a sudden Brenda, Sean's wife, says: "Would you like to stay here?" So he moved there and if he had happiness in Manchester this was it, this was his home from home.

'Liam would write or telephone the family two doors from us and sent Mammy £3 every week. He never forgot his mum.

'Until he went to the Dolans one of the problems he had was how he spent the days. He would train all morning and then finish about 1 pm and go to the pictures in town, but he got fed up with that. He would go to Mass, of course, and he was very friendly with Father Mulholland, but the afternoons were a terrible drag.'

United apart, Home Farm was Liam's only club and unlike his brothers he never attracted a single offer from a

League of Ireland club before United signed him in 1953. They had gone to Dublin to look at Vinny Ryan, a gifted team-mate of Whelan's at Home Farm. As so often happens, however, Ryan didn't perform on the day and Billy Behan, Ireland's scout in the south of the country, went back to Manchester with Liam's signature on a registration form.

When he did arrive in Manchester his countryman Johnny Carey had given him a first, valued piece of advice, and only half in jest.

'Hold on for your given name as long you can because for sure they will be calling you something else soon,' he advised the shy seventeen year old. Johnny Carey had become Jackie in Mancunian parlance and, sure enough, Liam soon became Billy, a state of affairs he bore with typical good grace and humour.

Whelan played only four games for his country, one of them the memorable 1–1 draw against England at Dalymount Park in May 1957, in a team that contained the future United captain, Noel Cantwell.

Liam left an indelible mark on that match. Once asked who he rated as the greatest English player of all time, Cantwell said: 'I never played with Duncan Edwards, but I played against him in perhaps the most famous World Cup game ever staged in Dublin and Liam Whelan nutmegged Duncan Edwards twice. I don't think Duncan was best pleased about that.'

Munich robbed Ireland of Liam's talents for ever, but he should have had a fifth game. He was selected for a match against the-then World Cup holders, West Germany, in Dublin on 25 November 1956, but the Irish management omitted to tell Busby that players who turned out for their clubs the previous day would automatically be replaced in the national team, even for a friendly. When Whelan arrived at the team hotel on the morning of the game, he was told his place had gone to Noel Peyton of Shamrock Rovers. Burying his disappointment, Liam went home to Cabra, returned to Dalymount Park in the afternoon, and paid to watch his countrymen beat the world champions 3–0.

Because of his quiet, devout nature, many people believed Whelan was as well suited to the priesthood as life as a footballer, but he did have a girlfriend in Dublin, Ruby, and two adoring female fans in Manchester.

'He was to be married that June 1958, to my friend Ruby McCullagh,' says sister Rita. 'I worked with her at the biscuit factory and he met her through me. Ruby was almost twenty-one and he had known her for two or three years. Beryl Townsend and Mary Mooney in Manchester also took a shine to Liam. Mary wrote to Mammy after Liam died and over the years they kept it going. Mary and Beryl sent postal orders on the anniversary, or on Liam's birthday or at Christmas to get flowers for Mass and that went on until 1996 when Mammy died. But they continued to write to me. We had this researcher for *The Gay Byrne Show* round once and he was saying how fantastic it was that this correspondence should go on for forty years, although we never met them, and had never even spoken to them on the phone.

'The researcher got Beryl's phone number and she came on the programme. Both of them never married, like me. Mary died about two years ago and I still don't know what she looked like, but we meet Beryl every time we go over. At the Cup Final of 1957, I was with Ruby when the game was over and Jackie Blanchflower's wife began to cry, she felt that Jackie having to go in goal had cost them the game.

'Liam cried as well. I can close my eyes now and still see him waving at me and Mammy from the Wembley pitch.

'At the Callista tournament back home in Dublin, just after the Wembley final, he wanted to go in goal. I told him the kids want to see you in the outfield, not in goal. Then as they played *Amrhan na bhFiann*, the anthem, Liam said: "Sure, this is better than Wembley." And he said later: "At least we won one final."'

Ireland, a small country with limited sporting resources, has always embraced its heroes wholeheartedly and that support recognizes few distinctions. Irish fans, north and south, will travel anywhere and to any venue to support a countryman or woman. Some of the green-bedecked thousands who flock to Lansdowne Road for international rugby or football were also in Paris in the summer of 1987 to see Stephen Roche clinch his only Tour de France victory, Barcelona in 1992 to cheer Michael Carruth on to his welterweight boxing gold and Atlanta in 1996 to see Michelle Smith swim her way to three gold medals. When Smith was later discredited as a drug-taker, the overriding emotion in Ireland was one of hurt, rather than outrage.

This wholehearted and indiscriminate loyalty, however, has its price and for Liam Whelan, as it is still for many Irish youngsters leaving home at an early age, the fear that they lived with every day was that they might let family, or country, down.

'Liam would take it very hard if he was not playing well,' says Christy. 'At one time when things got really bad and the crowd was on his back he even went and asked Mr Busby to leave him out of the team.'

Like his modern-day United counterpart John O'Shea, Whelan could look less than adroit, clumsy even, on the ball. Like O'Shea, he also lacked pace. Occasionally the Old Trafford crowd would lose patience, believing that the relaxed air was simply hesitancy. The barracking he occasionally suffered at Old Trafford affected him deeply and baffled his brothers, who have few doubts about his talent. For more discriminating fans, too, Whelan had plainly been blessed with extraordinary gifts. He possessed the knack of ghosting past an opponent, was a master of the nutmeg, a push of the ball through a flummoxed opponent's legs, and although most of the striking responsibilities were in the hands of Taylor and Dennis Viollet, he was deadly in front of goal. The twenty-six goals in thirty-nine senior outings in the championship-winning season of 1956–57 and his Division One total of forty-three in seventy-nine senior appearances, a remarkable strike rate for a midfielder, says just about everything. As John Whelan, a fine footballer in his own right for Drumcondra among other League of Ireland clubs, quite rightly points out: 'Ruud van Nistelrooy equalled Liam's record of eight consecutive goals for United in 2002–3, but Liam was never given any penalties to take in 56–57.' Christy adds: 'Bobby Charlton wanted to be the best player in the world but didn't think he would be while Liam was around.'

Irish football fans, of a certain vintage at least, have no hesitation in placing Liam alongside Peter Doherty, John Giles and Liam Brady in the hall of fame of great home-bred midfielders. And like every other player who died at Munich, the best undoubtedly lay ahead.

'You look at his record and discover that in ninety-six all-competition appearances for Manchester United he hit the target fifty-two times,' says Derek Dougan, the former Northern Ireland international. 'That's a phenomenal strike rate for an inside-forward, all the more so because he achieved it right at the start of his career.'

When the Elizabethan ran out of runway at Reim airport it ploughed through the perimeter fence and across a road. The port wing hit the house Thain had spotted ahead, the wing and part of the tail were torn off and the house, with the tail embedded in it, caught fire. A tree impaled the port side of the cockpit and the starboard side of the fuselage hit a wooden hut inside which a truck, filled with tyres and fuel, exploded.

Inside the plane, there was bedlam. Gregg said: 'I thought I was going to die. I braced myself and waited for the end. In the blackness, I thought I had died, but then I felt something trickling down my forehead and in my nose. I put my hand to my face and felt the warmth of blood. I began to crawl towards the hole in the aircraft. The first person I saw was Bert Whalley, lying in the snow, eyes wide open. He was dead. I thought, my God, I'm the only one alive, but then the captain appeared with a little fire extinguisher and bellowed, "Run, you silly bugger, she's going to blow." At that moment I heard a child cry. I crawled back into the plane, scrambling over the bodies in the dark, before I found the baby. Suddenly, a pile of rubbish erupted and out of it the child's mother appeared. I shoved her past me and out of the plane.

'I made my way outside and Bobby Charlton and Dennis Viollet were laying there, motionless. Then I saw Matt Busby, sitting twenty-five yards away. I went back to the front of the plane where the card school had been cut in two. I found Roger Byrne and Jackie Blanchflower in a deep pool of water.'

Rescue was slow to arrive and there were no ambulances or fire-fighters on the scene. 'Eventually,' Gregg recalled, 'a guy turned up in a coal van, and we got Jackie in and little Johnny Berry and the boss. We got into the van, with pieces of coal rolling about, and set off for the hospital.'

All the passengers, living and dead, were taken to Munich's Rechts der Isar hospital, where Gregg and Foulkes were left sitting in armchairs, wrapped in blankets. Eventually, the British consul took them from the hospital to the Stakus Hotel, where Foulkes sipped at a whisky for the first time and puffed at a first cigarette, supplied by Gregg.

The next day both men returned to the scene of the crash, standing in the detritus as the authorities combed the wreckage and photographers captured their numbed and haunted features. Inside the pulverized fuselage the rescuers found a brown paper bag containing an apple, an orange, a quarter of tea and two pounds of sugar, packed for Eddie Colman by his mother, Liz.

Back home, first news of the tragedy came via tele-printer: 'Manchester United aircraft crashed on take-off . . .

heavy loss of life feared.' The BBC interrupted its after-noon programmes to broadcast news flashes, all of them overtaking the local newspapers, whose coverage was already out of date. The news of the crash was all over the front pages of the *Manchester Evening News* and the *Chronicle* but, because the back pages had been done overnight, Tom Jackson's match report was the splash, including the forecast that 'United will never have a tougher fight than this'. On the same page Roger Byrne mused, in his ghost-written column, over the likely semi-final opponents and his preference for the defending champions Real Madrid. The reality, however, was on page one where massive headlines announced that twenty-one were already dead with four others critically injured.

The survivors' families were also acquainted with the awful news in varying ways. Sandy Busby was at Victoria Station in the city centre after arriving back from training at Blackburn Rovers, his club. A team-mate, Paddy Kennedy, was with him and Kennedy said: 'Have you seen the placards? It says United in air crash.'

'I dived for the phone at the station,' says Sandy. 'Mam said: "Get home straight away." I jumped into a taxi, and it was only when I got home that I realized the seriousness of it all. People were calling in, and the phone never stopped ringing. Frank Swift lived round the corner from us on Kings Road and his wife and daughter and another sportswriter, Henry Rose's girlfriend, came round. The news came through about Frank, then Henry, and his girl went into hysterics. In the meantime, my mum had gone into like a semi-coma. She was looking into the fire and no one could get any reaction from her. She wasn't talking or anything. I'd gone upstairs to my bedroom, and although I'm not a great religious person I started praying. Just then my uncle shouts upstairs: "Sandy, he's alive, he's alive." All of a sudden my mother came out of this trance and basically took over things.

'We knew then Tom Curry had died, so she sent me round to his house. Then Mum started arrangements to head off to Munich the following morning and we flew from Ringway, via Paris, and there were other relatives, and Jimmy Murphy on the plane. Scanny and Viollet's wife were on the flight although some had apparently had problems in Paris because they didn't have passports. But the immigration let them fly anyway. In Munich we took a taxi to the Hotel Metropol which was packed with press, and then on to the hospital.'

The scene that greeted the families of the survivors in the Rechts der Isar Hospital was one of total devastation. Busby and Duncan Edwards were in oxygen tents, Charlton's head was bandaged, and Jackie Blanchflower had suffered multiple injuries. His arm had been almost severed. Albert Scanlon was unconscious with a fractured skull, and Dennis Viollet had a gashed head and facial injuries. Goalkeeper Ray Wood's face was also badly cut and he had concussion and Ken Morgans and Johnny Berry lay in their beds as if dead. But the full horror of Munich sank in for the first time when one of the families asked a nurse where the rest of the players were. The nurse replied: 'Others? There are no others, they are all here.'

Roger Byrne, Geoff Bent, Mark Jones, David Pegg, Liam Whelan, Eddie Colman and Tommy Taylor had been killed instantly along with three of the backroom staff, the bird-like little secretary Crickmer and the genial coaching friends Tom Curry and Bert Whalley. The co-pilot Ken Rayment, who had to be cut from the aircraft cockpit, was to die in hospital later after a fight for life as prolonged as that of Edwards.

'I walked in the ward and saw an old grey man in the first bed and it was only when I got a bit further on I realized it was me dad,' says Sandy Busby. 'They gave him the last rites twice.'

The bodies were flown home and lay overnight in the gym at Old Trafford, journalists Tom Jackson and Alf Clarke, Crickmer, Curry, Whalley, Mark Jones, Roger Byrne, Geoff Bent, Tommy Taylor and Eddie Colman. Two policemen guarded the coffins and Omo and Daz, the cleaning ladies who a week earlier had been brewing tea for the Babes and looking after their laundry, now had the task of polishing their caskets. Then came the funerals, the memorial services and the two minutes of silence at matches everywhere. 'United will go on,' proclaimed the chairman Harold Hardman. They would go on, but how, no one seemed to know. As well as players, staff and press, the obituaries were already being written for a football club.

Another team died at Munich, as Harry Gregg will remind anyone who cares to listen. 'Everyone goes on about the players, but what about the other people who died? What about the journalists, the steward, the dead pilot and James Thain, who didn't die there but was certainly killed a little bit?'

Gregg is right that the other dead at Munich – eight sports writers, co-pilot Ken Rayment, Tommy Cable the steward, Manchester businessman Willie Satinoff and two other passengers – should not be forgotten, but generally are. But the truth about any tragedy on a grand scale is that the most famous are remembered first. Only the most devoted music fan can name the others in the plane crash that killed Buddy Holly almost twelve months to the day after Munich. 2 February 1959 will always be recalled as the day Holly died, not Richie Valens or the Big Bopper.

The dead sportswriters, eight of the nine on board, had their own audience and their own fame and Alf Clarke, Don Davies, George Follows, Tom Jackson, Archie

Ledbrooke, Henry Rose, Eric Thompson and the former England goalkeeper Frank Swift a rapport with their public that is seldom seen today. The players trusted them, too, probably because these journalists, the cream of the north's sportswriters in the days when Manchester was a major publishing centre, were always able to find the means to tread the fine line between the need to produce stories and the demands of deadlines and the possibility of causing offence to their subjects.

Now they were the news.

Only Frank Taylor of the *News Chronicle* lived to tell the tale, recovering from massive injuries which kept him in hospital for five months and even surviving the publication of his own obituary, mistakenly published in his own newspaper, and written by a young sportswriter called Ian Wooldridge. Des Hackett, the larger-than-life, bowler-hatted *Daily Express* writer performed the same function for Rose, beginning his piece on the day of his colleague's funeral on a dank Manchester day: 'Even the skies wept for Henry Rose today . . .'

Of the players, too, the name of Geoff Bent is invariably the last recalled and of the triumvirate of Manchester Babes to die at Munich, the most unfortunate was undoubtedly Eddie Colman's fellow Salfordian. Born in similar circumstances to Colman, and like Colman an only child, Bent was brought up in Jacksons Buildings in Irlams o' th' Height where a welcoming sign in the front room said 'Home, Sweet Home', Bent was twenty-five and a relative senior by the time of the crash and had already suffered two broken legs in a United career that never really caught fire, mainly because he was understudy at left-back to the undroppable Byrne. He had captained Salford Schoolboys when they had won the English School's Trophy in 1947 and had been picked up by United a year later. Tall, well built and a strong tackler, it was felt he would eventually take over from John Aston at left-back, until Byrne made his well-publicized switch from the wing to the number three shirt. Bent would, unarguably, have been an automatic choice at almost any other club in the country, but ultimately his first-team appearances were limited to twelve following his debut against Burnley at Turf Moor on 11 December 1954. Most of his Old Trafford career was spent in the reserves, often alongside seven or eight internationals, a state of affairs he accepted with characteristic good grace and humour. 'Why don't you come and join the real team?' he would chide Byrne. Bent, half-heartedly admittedly, twice asked Busby for a move, only to be told he was too valuable to the squad to be allowed to leave and the arrival of his daughter, Karen, late in 1957 and the offer of a club house on King's Road finally settled him.

Geoff Bent shouldn't have gone to Belgrade. Like his captain he was a notoriously bad flier, suffering from nose bleeds at even modest altitudes. He had welcomed the news that he would be staying at home with his wife Marion and five-month-old Karen when the team sheet was pinned up in the first-team dressing room at Old Trafford. Then Byrne suffered a slight strain in the match at Highbury and Busby told the unwilling reserve he would have to go to Belgrade as cover. In the event, Byrne was fit to face the Yugoslavs and Bent flew to his death simply as a passenger. Later, Busby came the closest ever to admitting guilt over Munich when he went to visit Marion, telling her that he should have told the pilots to abort the third, final attempt at takeoff.

Marion Bent, according to Harry Gregg, became one of the unsung heroes of the post-disaster United. Left with a baby daughter to bring up and with little in the way of recompense for the next four decades until the club finally remembered their duties to the families of the dead, Marion was not the type to broadcast her woes to the world. Gregg says, with something close to anger: 'I was at the post-match function at Bolton on the fortieth anniversary and I saw Marion standing outside with her daughter. She told me she didn't feel she had the right to be there. Hadn't the right! I took her inside and sat her down with some of the other wives she had been close to when Geoff was alive.'

In all, twenty-three passengers had died at Munich, but there was a measure of hope for everyone connected with the club in the knowledge that Busby and a number of players had survived. The club had to look ahead. Back in St Attracta Road in Dublin, it was Mrs Whelan who first recognized that their duty now lay to the living.

'I can see her now,' says her daughter Rita. 'I can still see Mammy, cleaning out the fire at home as she turned to me and said: "Won't you look after Ruby? Please, look after Ruby."'

6

DUNCANVILLE

If the men and women on the terraces of football grounds nourish their own dreams and ambitions within the bodies of the players they idolize, then Duncan Edwards's recovery from injuries that had brutalized that superb athlete's physique became a fundamental for millions in the days following Munich. Even more so for the fans of United and the people of Manchester, for the overwhelming fear was that on the fate of Edwards hinged the fate of the club. If he died, so did Manchester United.

Even for those who had never seen him play and evinced little interest in football, the player's fight for life against the most appalling odds took on a symbolism which went far beyond the confines of sport. His injuries included damaged kidneys, broken ribs, a collapsed lung, broken pelvis, and multiple fractures of the right thigh. His sufferings in the Rechts der Isar Hospital were of biblical proportions.

His family and friends suffered, too, as the daily prognosis rose from hopeless to hopeful and back again every twenty-four hours; first he rallied, then relapsed. The likelihood was that even if he had lived he would have been crippled for life and never played football again.

'The strength of Duncan was unbelievable,' says Sandy Busby who had accompanied his mother Jean, sister Sheena and Duncan's fiancée Molly Leach to Munich the day after the crash. 'His body had been crushed. Everything was crushed and there he was fighting. Molly was not religious, not at all, but she went to church in Munich to pray for him.'

When Murphy arrived, Edwards opened his eyes long enough to recognize the distraught Welshman. He demanded to know the time of kick-off on Saturday and when he was told 'three o'clock, the usual time, son' the player echoed the exhortation Murphy employed in the dressing room at the end of every team talk before every United match.

'Get stuck in,' he said.

Duncan Edwards died at 2.15 am on Friday 21 February, fifteen long days and nights after the crash.

The flickering black-and-white newsreel captures him for ever, all tousled fair hair and muscle, bare-foot in white shirt and shorts, nimbly vaulting the South Stand picket fencing for the benefit of the camera and smiling into the lens. A beguiling mixture of innocence and seeming naivety, he blushed when his team-mates pulled his leg – usually about his Midlands accent and his birthplace of 'Dood-lie' – and as a boy kept pigeons and rabbits and liked fishing and hop-picking. But on his first visit as an England international to Hampden Park in April 1956, Edwards kicked the little native icon Bobby Johnstone up in the air in front of 100,000 scandalized, screaming Scots and also warned the legendary Newcastle and England centre-forward Jackie Milburn before a Division One match: 'I don't care about reputations, they mean nothing to me. Any bother from you and I'll boot you over the stand.' Afterwards, he shook the bemused Milburn by the hand, and told him: 'Thanks for the game, chief.' He called everyone chief. In turn, they called him Brush, because of his insistence on tidiness.

He was born on 1 October 1936, at 23, Malvern Crescent in Dudley before his parents, Sarah and Gladstone, moved to Priory Estate, parts of which are still considered the roughest and most deprived in the Midlands.

Duncan was ten when a sister, christened Carol Anne, died from meningitis at the age of fourteen weeks; he was to grow up healthy and strong and with good genes possibly inherited from his mum who, when she died in 2003 was ninety-three years old. His father played football at amateur level and an uncle was on Bolton's books in the early Thirties and also represented England.

'Duncan the athlete came out of his mum,' says Scanlon.

'There was one time when we were doing laps before Jimmy and Bert came out and there was a lad called Alan Rhodes there. He was a full-back from Chesterfield, but he was also a gymnast, and could do double somersaults. He'd run down the track and do it. Course, Duncan has to have a go. He falls flat on his arse the first time; the second time he does it, no problem.'

Just as David Pegg was playing on the spare ground surrounding his home in Highfields, Doncaster, Albert Scanlon and Eddie Colman on the bombed-out sites of Manchester and Salford and Bobby Charlton in the back streets of Ashington in Co Durham, Duncan was kicking a ball about from an early age, usually around Netherton or Priory Parks. He played for Priory Road junior school, bossing the other boys around and at the age of eleven a watching schoolteacher wrote to a friend that he had seen a schoolboy 'who would one day play for England'.

In 1948, at the age of twelve, Edwards moved into secondary school at Wolverhampton Street, captaining the school side, and then into the Dudley Schools side. From then on it was an unstoppable upward curve: Worcester County, Birmingham and District and England Schools. It was obvious that such precocity would soon attract attention and the Edwardses soon found themselves being courted by a host of football clubs. Many in Dudley assumed Duncan would head for his 'local' team, Wolverhampton Wanderers, but they were left standing by the United talent-gathering machine.

Late in 1948 a hastily scribbled note arrived on Busby's desk from his Midlands scout Jack O'Brien, who wrote: 'Have today seen a schoolboy who merits special watching. His name is Duncan Edwards of Dudley. Instructions please.'

Busby relayed the message to Bert Whalley and Jimmy Murphy, instructing them: 'Please arrange special watch immediately – MB' after which a record of the youngster's progress was card-indexed by Alma George in Busby's office. His character, sportsmanship and bearing on the field were also studied, Murphy spoke to his teachers and finally went to see his father and mother. By 1952, Wolves were said to be closing in and United took no chances. Late on 1 June, Bert Whalley chauffeured Murphy, who did not drive, through the night, arriving at the Edwards's home in the early hours. The sleep-befuddled Edwards signed there and then, in his pyjamas.

Busby was always unwilling later to categorize his 'greatest ever' at Old Trafford, but the name of Duncan Edwards would always produce a sparkle in the old man's eyes long after he had left the club.

For Busby, Duncan was 'the player who had everything. He was so big, so strong, and so confident. And so young.

We used to look at players in training to see if we might have to get them to concentrate more on their kicking, perhaps, or their heading or ball control, whatever. We looked at Duncan, right at the start, and gave up trying to spot flaws in his game.

'Apart from anything else, he could move upfield and lash in goals when we needed them. John Charles was a giant of a player, a giant with great skill. But as a player he didn't have as much as Duncan. He used to move up the field, brushing players aside. Nothing could stop and nothing unnerved him.

'The bigger the occasion, the better he liked it. He had no nerves before a game. He was like George Best in that respect. While other players would have to be pacing up and down a dressing room, rubbing their legs, doing exercises and looking for ways to pass the time, Duncan, and George later, was always calm. They would glance through a programme or get changed casually and wait without a trace of tension.'

When Busby brought centre-half Ronnie Cope into the team for the final match at Highbury in February 1958, the manager had no hesitation in asking Edwards, a boy himself, 'to keep an eye on him' in the manner of a veteran professional.

'He was a good type of lad, too,' added Busby. 'Even in those days, when football followers were not what they became later with regard to wanting to be with players socially, you still had people who waited for them. But Duncan did not want to know about the high life. He just wanted to play and go to his digs or go home. He lived for his football.'

His death impacted into many areas, and not just among the fans smitten by his youthful enthusiasm epitomized by those bounding leaps down the tunnel on to the field and an all-embracing influence on every game he played, from taking every free-kick, every corner to goal-scoring and defending.

His former England team-mate, Jimmy Armfield, has no hesitation in saying that the death of Edwards, combined with the simultaneous loss of Roger Byrne and Tommy Taylor, struck England a blow from which it took almost a decade to recover and cost them the World Cup in Sweden in 1958 and, possibly, the following one in Chile.

Armfield, who after Munich was to name his eldest son Duncan in an act of homage mirrored in thousands of households, says: 'He was a one-off and he grew up very quickly, he was physically mature at eighteen. When he first appeared for Young England, the opposition didn't dare tackle him. They just backed off. He was a super bloke but he liked his own way and could be fiery. But there is no doubt in my mind that with Byrne, Edwards and Taylor in the team we would have won the World Cup in Sweden in 1958 and in South America four years later. England could have had a hat-trick of World Cup wins.

Munich robbed us of three of the greatest players of any era, not just the Babes era.'

The former England manager Terry Venables was standing in the old Clock End at Highbury with his father, Fred, when United bade their unforgettable farewell to England five days before Munich. Venables, who had just turned fifteen years old at the time, had already lost his heart to the young Edwards. He recalled: 'When I was growing up, there was no televised football to speak of, and if you wanted to see a particular player or team, it meant going to one of their matches. It was February 1958 and United had just caused a stir by beating Bolton 7–2, and everyone was talking about Duncan Edwards. So I persuaded my dad to come with me to Highbury to see United play Arsenal. It was an unusual trip for two committed Spurs fans, and a day I will never forget. It took Duncan Edwards less than ten minutes to show us what all the fuss was about. I remember I was a bit disappointed that United weren't at full strength with the Belgrade tie ahead, but it was still a hell of a team, with a forward line that included Bobby Charlton, Tommy Taylor and Dennis Viollet, supported from half-back by Eddie Colman and the man I couldn't take my eyes off, Duncan.

'Jack Kelsey, a legend at Highbury, was in goal for Arsenal but, good as he was, he was beaten all the way when Duncan opened the scoring with a cracking shot. That was my moment. We had travelled in to see him and, with the latecomers still arriving, he had me turning to my dad with a "Did you see that?" look. Edwards had taken a pass from Viollet and strode forward like an unstoppable giant before shooting past Kelsey from twenty-five yards. There were eight more goals in a fantastic match, but Duncan's, and his overall performance, are all I really remember. Afterwards, I just couldn't get it out of my head how good United were. Duncan was marvellous. Everything he did comes back to me as if it was yesterday. Such strength, such poise. We are talking about a long time ago, but I can still see him, and that tremendous power of his, even now.'

Like so many, Edwards left an indelible impression on Venables. A man not given to unwarranted sentiment, many years later he was to hang an oil painting of 'my hero and inspiration' in the restaurant at his London club, Scribes West. He is also happy to utter what many will regard as heresy: 'Duncan Edwards played in the same position, number six, as Bobby Moore and in the summer of 1966 would have been only twenty-nine. How could you ever pick Moore, great player though he was, ahead of Duncan?'

It was certainly a sentiment shared with Moore himself, who was to write in his autobiography: 'I once played truant from school to watch Duncan play at White Hart Lane. He put two past Tottenham. He was the Rock of Gibraltar at the back, dynamite coming forward. There will never be another player like him. Duncan's death was the greatest tragedy of the United air crash.

'I cried when I heard. I was visiting Malcolm Allison and Noel Cantwell (West Ham team-mates) and we all sat there crying, two grown men and me.'

As Moore and Venables realized at once, the tragedy of Duncan Edwards – more so even than his talented team-mates – was that of a prodigy stillborn, a talent unfulfilled.

His Old Trafford and England team-mates also acknowledged his gifts, but in the manner of groups of young men everywhere kept his feet on the ground with a mixture of laddish banter and irreverent piss-take.

'Coming back on the train from that last Arsenal game the lads were taking the mickey out of him without mercy,' says Harry Gregg. 'There had been talk and gossip going on about Billy Wright moving from centre-half and captain and all the lads were ribbing Duncan about taking over, calling him the blue-eyed boy and everything. I remember Duncan was so embarrassed. He was blushing and saying: "Mark [Jones] is a far better centre-half than me. He should be in."'

The United players were not alone in attempting to keep Duncan from becoming too big for his football boots.

Albert Scanlon says: 'After training we used to play a practice game. Bill Inglis, who liked to sneak off somewhere quiet for a smoke, says to us: "Go out there and do some laps until I'm ready for you." So Duncan puts his top on, two towels round his neck, and sets off. We did a few laps and then went back to the game. That's when we realized they were one short, and of course it's Duncan. He's still out there running. When he finally appears after about thirty minutes Bill says: "Where the hell have you been?" and Duncan says: "No one told me to stop." He even tried smoking once, just cos everyone else seemed to do it at Old Trafford.'

'Duncan only wanted one thing and that was to play football,' says Harry Gregg. 'At the end of every training session he would argue that we hadn't done enough yet. He didn't want to go in.'

Despite his apparent lack of guile, Edwards was well aware of the commercial opportunities his name and talent afforded him; in so many ways he was far ahead of his time. He had endorsed Dextrosol glucose tablets acclaiming a 'natural source of energy you can rely on anytime and anywhere' – not that he ever appeared to need any extra help – and had already acquired sponsored transport, a Raleigh racing bike. He was paid four pounds ten shillings a week by the *Manchester Evening Chronicle* for a newspaper column in the *Saturday Pink* and by the age of twenty-one had written a best-selling instructional book entitled *Tackle Soccer This Way*. Wise and far-sighted beyond his years he told one journalist: 'You can't live for ever on cheers, it's what you have in the bank at the end of the day that counts. People forget very quickly and I don't want to become like some of the old timers wearing tattered caps and cadging for tickets outside the grounds.'

As it happened, fate spared Edwards decrepitude and poverty, but also ensured that people would never forget.

His stature since his death has grown rather than diminished. Commentators of the period, and almost everyone since, use the same descriptions of him: a colossus, legs like tree trunks, barrel-chested, a freak of nature, and yet he stood just 5 ft 10 in and weighed under thirteen stones, big for a Fifties footballer perhaps, but small for a colossus.

'The biggest man in that team was me,' says Harry Gregg. 'I was around 13 st 10 lb, then Mark Jones and Tommy Taylor followed me. Duncan, topside, was 5 ft 10 in. and under thirteen stones, but he was square-built. Alongside wee Eddie, of course, he looked enormous.'

By the time he died at the age of twenty-one he had won eighteen England caps and was being hailed as one of the greatest players of all time. Some contemporaries, however, still urge restraint when considering Edwards.

'Five or six years ago I was on a radio programme and I was asked to pick my best team ever,' says Scanlon. 'At wing-half, I know who you are going to say, but was he the best? My choice played for Manchester City, he captained them, and his name was Roy Paul.'

Doherty adds: 'I remember Duncan first arriving. He was a big, strong lad and initially very quiet. It was obvious he was a huge talent, but did he have more than little Eddie? People talk as if he were a giant, but he wasn't; he was the same size as me. Most of the people who write about him never saw him.'

Whether they saw him or not, Edwards touched the psyche of every generation and, seemingly every nationality, often in inexplicable fashion. Half a century on, the reverence for him remains undiminished, particularly in a small town in England's Black Country.

Even the residents will admit that Dudley has seen better days. The grimy nail of a finger that extends from rural Worcestershire into the Black Country of the English Midlands, Dudley was once, with neighbouring Tipton, Briery Hill and Bilston, part of a flourishing quartet of productive steelworks towns in an area that, like South Wales and Yorkshire, once boasted pride in a commodity.

This pride was all but destroyed in the late Eighties when, one by one, the massive furnaces were stilled. Pledges from a series of governments and job-creating agencies proved to be empty and Dudley now is a depressed and depressing area of run-down corner pubs, low-grade supermarkets, high-rise blocks of flats and shops that offer to cash DHS cheques. A reggae group from the area, symbolically and sardonically, named themselves UB40 after the official designation of the unemployment benefit form, and the building of a massive new shopping centre five miles away at Merry Hill further decimated the Dudley economy.

The town does have some minor claims to fame. Lenny Henry, the comedian, Sue Lawley, the television presenter, film director James Whale and current Bolton Wanderers manager Sam Allardyce were all born in Dudley and the conspirators behind the Gunpowder Plot hid in its vast limestone caves. The anchor, chain and glassware used on the *Titanic* were made there and Dudley's natural resources put the town at the forefront of steel and glassware production in the industrial revolution.

There is a tribalism about the West Midlands, probably only found elsewhere in South Wales, and Dudley even has a dialect of its own; the accent here is subtly different from the surrounding towns, different even from Quarry Bank ten miles away. In Dudley you don't go home, you go 'wum'; a friend is an 'alloy' (this from the partisanships forged in the steel industry) and to cry a lot is known as 'blartin'. The common language of the area, however, is football, and the name of Duncan Edwards.

'I think after the steelworks closed the people were desperate to find pride in something,' says journalist Paul Greaves who was born at Quarry Bank and whose father, Fred, worked for thirty years in the local steelworks. Greaves began his career on the local evening paper, the *Express and Star* and he says now: 'I am not saying they did not know about Duncan before but in the late Eighties and early Nineties when things began to get really bad I think they began to treasure his memory a bit more.'

Greaves is also convinced that the loss of Edwards to Manchester United was a body blow from which football in the Midlands failed to recover.

'If you think about it, Wolves was the logical place for him to go and in those days they were very successful. Since then, it has all been downhill. Villa, Birmingham and West Brom have had their moments since, but five major football clubs in one area should have achieved a lot more.

'You can't say that one man would have made all that difference, but Duncan playing on his home land would certainly have attracted other youngsters. As it is, what have Wolves done since the late Fifties? My dad compared everyone to Duncan, always to their detriment. "He's all right, but he's no Duncan Edwards, is he?" he would say.'

Nowadays, it could be argued that Duncan Edwards is Dudley's main tourist attraction; there is a pub named after him close by the Priory estate, a statue in the centre of the town, a museum in the local leisure centre and his grave has become a place of pilgrimage for football fans of every persuasion. Local schoolchildren still compete for a Duncan Edwards Trophy. The town in many ways is a huge shrine to Edwards and if the local council chose to rename Dudley Duncanville no one would be in the least surprised.

On 6 February 2003, forty-five years after the disaster, the skies above the streets of Dudley were a sheet of unbroken grey and overnight snow was still melting in the gutters of the town's streets. There was unconditional warmth to strangers, however, whenever the name was mentioned.

The Duncan Edwards pub stands 500 yards from Elm Road, where Edwards spent much of his childhood. It was once known as the Wren's Nest, but landlord Matthew Wilkinson has few doubts which is the more fitting name.

When Wilkinson took over the licence, there were requests for help to Manchester United, all of which have gone unheeded.

He says: 'We wrote two letters three months before Christmas to Old Trafford asking for their support in what we were trying to do but we have had nothing back at all, not even a letter of acknowledgement.'

United, however, long ago adopted a policy of never passing on mementoes that could be sold, even autographed shirts. When the former Busby Babe Dennis Viollet was dying in America, a request from the Manchester-based appeal fund for an autographed match ball to be auctioned off to raise funds was also refused.

That hasn't stopped the worshippers in a Dudley pub, however.

Barmaid Brenda Wilson, who has worked there for thirteen years, says: 'Loads of people come here as a kind of pilgrimage to Duncan. They ask the way to the church with the stained-glass windows and they ask the way to the grave. A coachload of United fans came a few weeks back and although I am not much up on football, because people who come here are always asking about Duncan I am learning.'

Rino Gambone is a United fan of Italian extraction who was born in Bolsover, Derbyshire two years before Munich. His parents, Armando and Rosa, are from the southern Italian province of Avelino which is inland from Naples.

'I have been a football fan for as long as I can remember and growing up in an Italian household a lot of the talk was about soccer,' says Gambone. 'I remember hearing about the FC Torino players who died in an air crash in 1949 when they were coming home from a game. Most of them in our household supported Internazionale, but I supported Torino then, I don't know why.'

The Gambone family moved to Wolverhampton, which has a massive Italian community, in the early Sixties and Rino's original fealties belonged to Molineux where he would be taken by an uncle.

'Then, when I was around nine years old, there was this teacher at Stonefield Primary School in Bilston and his name was Mr Edwards. He reckoned his cousin was this lad called Duncan Edwards and he said Duncan would have been the greatest football player the world had ever seen if he had not been killed as a result of the Munich air disaster. That made me think.

'Early on, my heroes were big strong centre-forwards like Derek Dougan of Wolves or Jeff Astle who played for West Brom, but I kept thinking about this Duncan Edwards who would have been the greatest of them all. I was one of those lads who would kick a football from morning till night, usually with my brothers and my mates in Ladymoor in Bilston and at Broadlanes School football pitch from about 1960 onwards. I fancied myself as a bit of a Denis Law.'

Like many of the current and far-flung United support, Rino Gambone became a fan almost by proxy.

'It wasn't until the late Sixties that I became hooked on them. It was around the time that travelling United fans started making a name for themselves in the newspapers. It was the aura, the magic of United being in town. People would hitch-hike from all over the country to follow United. I was there in Whitmore Reans, which was a dull, uncelebrated place just outside of Wolverhampton town centre and then United would come.

'There would be thousands of girls, hitch-hikers, people in cars all flooding into town and it was just a fantastic buzz. It was big, it was colourful, the fans were wearing scarves around all parts of their bodies. There were mods, greebos, bell-bottom wearers and in those days we were all dressed by our dads. The first United game I went to was in 1968 at West Brom, it was a night game and United lost 6–3.

'I was twelve then at that game at the Hawthorns and there were 60,000 inside the stadium and it seemed like about 40,000 outside. It was just magical.

'Then I started to hear more and more about the club's history and about Munich and about Duncan. I often think about Duncan and I take flowers to his grave each year on 6 February because I can. I am lucky enough to live close by. I commemorate his death every year for the last few years. On Tuesday night, before the game against Birmingham around fifteen or twenty United fans arrived from Blackpool to go to the grave.'

The town cemetery is on Stourbridge Road where narrow, tarmacadamed paths take you to higher ground near some stark trees. The headstone has an ingrained picture of Duncan in football kit holding a ball above his head for a throw-in. An inscription reads: 'A Day Of Memory, Sad To Recall. Without Farewell, He Left Us All.' There are three flower stands, one of them in the shape of a football. Duncan's grave was once tended by his father, Gladstone, who after Munich took a job there.

On the day of Duncan's funeral 50,000 people lined the streets of the town and solemn, uniformed policemen saluted as the cortege drove slowly past.

'I was at the funeral and I knew Duncan,' says Pat Forrest who lives just off Stourbridge Road. 'He was two or three years younger than me and we went to Priory Junior which is just down the road. He went to

Wolverhampton Street Senior School and he would walk up the hill always heading a ball against the fence and kicking the ball down the street. I can still see him; always kicking or heading a ball. He were a decent lad and I remember the astonishment and the sadness when we heard about the crash and Duncan dying. People come from all over the world to see the window and the grave and I have met people from South Africa, Australia and all over England. We had even more come on the day Duncan would have been sixty years old and you could see the emotion when they stood in front of the window. Twenty-one and all his life in front of him.'

Like Pat Forrest and Rino Gambone in their own ways, Duncan's mother, Sarah Anne Edwards, known to all as Annie, was to be sustained by memories of the footballer.

Munich had left her devastated and she told family friends later: 'I'll never forget when Duncan died and they put his body in a chapel at the hospital. We linked arms, myself', my husband Gladstone, Matt Busby and his wife when we went in to see him. I can't begin to explain how I felt when I saw him. I expected his body to be laid out, but he was sitting upright on a chair. I went over and held him and kissed him.'

For the next half century Annie spent most of her time at home, reflecting on the past with the help of three framed photographs on the living-room wall.

There was one of Duncan in his army uniform, one with

his girlfriend Molly Leach, a Manchester girl he met on one of his afternoon trips to Ringway Airport and one of him in the United shirt, in which he made his senior debut at the age of fifteen years and 285 days, against Cardiff City in 1953. At eighteen, he became the youngest player ever to be picked for the full England team, the one which beat Scotland 7–2 at Wembley in April 1955, and a record beaten only by the then Everton wunderkid Wayne Rooney forty-eight years later.

Annie, who was too ill to be interviewed for this book, died, aged ninety-three, on 15 April 2003, grieving for her son to the last. Sir Bobby Charlton, Duncan's team-mate, joined hundreds of mourners at the funeral, the gesture spoiled – or enhanced depending on one's point of view – only by the Manchester United logo on his black coat. She was buried in the churchyard alongside Gladstone, her daughter Carol. and Duncan.

Manchester and the world recovered from Munich. Life had to go on. A few days after the crash, Roger Byrne's column in the *Manchester Evening News* had been replaced by one from the new captain Bill Foulkes whose first words to the *MEN* readership were: 'When I was young I used to dream of captaining a great team like Man United. Now my dream has come true – but I wish it hadn't.'

There were efforts, too, to establish the exact cause of the accident. In the House of Commons, the Minister of

Transport and Civil Aviation, revealed under questioning that under international agreement the responsibility for investigating these accidents rested with the Federal German Government. A senior inspector left for Munich to take part in that investigation as Britain's accredited representative. That investigation and its outcome were to prove highly contentious and damaging for the BEA pilot, Captain Thain, in particular.

Football went on, too, against the wishes of many. United chairman Harold Hardman had said: 'Even if it means being heavily defeated, we will carry on with the season's programme. We have a duty to the public and a duty to football to carry out.' The chairman added that the board would be meeting shortly to decide future policy. Alan Hardaker and the Football League had already taken that decision, however, and decided that the fixtures on the Saturday following the accident would be played, with the obvious exception of Manchester United's game with Wolves. A short silence was observed, flags at grounds flew at half mast, players wore black armbands, and reporters black ties. Hardaker said: 'The chairman of Manchester United, Mr Harold Hardman, has authorized me to say that, on behalf of the club, he wholeheartedly agreed with the management committee's decision to carry on with tomorrow's league programme. Mr Hardman asked that players should turn out and play the game in the normal way which would be their best way of paying tribute to the players concerned in the tragedy. He was confident that Mr Busby and all connected with the United club who lost their lives, or were injured, would wish it so.'

To which the obvious riposte was that none were in the fortunate position to take such a decision, a feeling underlined by Bert Tann, the manager of Bristol Rovers, who said: 'It smacks of complete disregard for the feelings of those who mourn . . . critics will say the need to make money transcends all other feelings.' Cliff Lloyd, secretary of the Players' Union, said that they had contacted the league after some players had told him that they would prefer not to play. He had asked the league if their decision could be reconsidered, but they gave their reasons why they had decided the matches should be played.

'We will abide by their decision,' said Lloyd.

The overwhelming concerns now were for the crash survivors. Could Charlton, Gregg, Foulkes and the rest of the players who had gone to Belgrade, recover sufficiently to play again? Would Busby be able to take over the reins and carry on? Would the mental scars prove too burdensome? The portents were not good.

When they moved him out of intensive care and up to a ward on the top floor of the hospital in the Rechts der Isar, some colour had returned to Busby's cheeks, coinciding with the first signs of spring outside.

'It was a sunny day and I suggested we could open the windows and wheel the bed on to the balcony,' says son Sandy. 'All you could see was sky and he shouted: "Get me back in, get me back in."'

It was clear that 6 February 1958 had left wounds that would be slow to heal, wounds that in some cases will never heal.

7

WHITE ROSES, RED CARNATIONS

John Doherty is not, as he admits, the most sentimental of men. One of the original Busby Babes, and one of Harry Gregg's Manchester Busby Babes at that, he was a skilled inside-forward with a shot whose velocity rivalled Bobby Charlton's. A former Manchester and Lancashire schools representative, he joined United as an amateur in 1950, signed professional forms in 1952 and made his first-team debut the same year.

His own playing career was finished by a knee injury at the age of twenty-three after Busby had shipped him out to Leicester City and while he was one of three members of the Munich testimonial committee of 1998, he insists: 'I don't get sentimental about all that because I am an old man now.'

Doherty, who smokes large cigars, is on first-name terms with most of the restaurant and bar staff in the Manchester hotel in which we met and is welcomed as one of the family at Old Trafford on match days, likes to come across as a hard-bitten ex-pro.

'Some of the lads who survived never played again, but what about me?' he demands. 'I was employed by United and my career was ended while I was playing for them. What's the difference? Everyone thinks they were top of the league come Munich but they weren't. As for the players, I don't know how long Pegg would have lasted with others around. Bill Foulkes's career would have been a lot shorter at Old Trafford without Munich. Shay Brennan wouldn't have had a career at Old Trafford but for Munich and there would never have been an Albert Quixall at United. Supporters will insist they would have won the league for the next ten years and they might have done. Then again, they might not.'

However hard he tries, Doherty cannot maintain his cynicism for long. The memories are too good, too fresh.

'The eight years at United will always be with me, from the Careys, Pearsons, Rowleys, to the Blanchflowers, Colmans and Taylors. There was a tremendous happy set-up at Old Trafford. Bill Foulkes was known as PB because he wasn't Popular Bill, but with the rest there were no factions at all and it was an incredible atmosphere there at the time. My eldest lad is called Mark after Mark Jones. He was a big, lovely fellow and every time I close my eyes I can always see Mark Jones's face. He was not a mate of mine, I was closer to the others, but he epitomized everything that was nice, everything that was good. He was a giant of a man and a giant of a human being. Big Mark was never really one of us. He was married and like an elder statesman with a pork pie hat and pipe. I loved him to bits.'

Jones, the elder statesman, was only twenty-four at the time of Munich but was everyone's favourite older brother among the United players. He wore a trilby hat, smoked a pipe and had the build of a cruiserweight boxer, an impression reinforced by the permanent scar tissue and taut skin around his eyebrows, like the cuts-prone heavyweight, Henry Cooper. He lived on the King's Road with his wife June, a Barnsley girl he had met when he was sixteen, and his infant son Gary, and had trained as a bricklayer before becoming a professional footballer.

He left Wombwell, Barnsley, in 1948 to cross the Pennines to Manchester and was already a captain of England Boys when he arrived. He signed professional forms in 1950 and was the archetypal stopper built in the manner of his predecessor, and boyhood hero, Allenby Chilton: broad-shouldered, strong in the air and uncompromising in the tackle. As he did with Bill Foulkes after him, Jimmy Murphy had hammered home the principles of centre-half play early on: 'Nothing fancy, just boot the bloody ball over the stand.'

Jones was to win two Championship medals with United,

and relished the physical challenge presented by opposing centre-forwards built on similar lines as himself. The match-ups between number nines like Nat Lofthouse of Bolton Wanderers and Sunderland's Trevor Ford and Jones and Foulkes were games within a game. He also had stern competition at Old Trafford, a continual battle for the centre-half spot with Jackie Blanchflower, who had been best man at his wedding. The Ulsterman edged selection for the 1957 FA Cup Final, but by the time of Munich, Jones had regained his place and was playing the best football of his career.

His team-mates christened him Dan Archer, after the radio soap patriarch, as much a reference to his rural habits, his love of shooting and country walks with his black Labrador and his fifty-five budgies. The birds were a passion. One match day Jones was late for the coach. Busby was furious, but his player explained: 'You should have gone without me. One of my budgies was ill and I'll not leave one of them for anything.' Jones, who owned a shotgun, also helped the secretary Walter Crickmer keep the pigeon population under control at the ground, much to the consternation of the Old Trafford apprentices. He was one of the few Babes who owned a car, a little Morris 1000, in which he would ferry round his wife June, pregnant with their daughter Lynn at the time of Munich, and two-year-old Gary. Shortly before the Munich crash he'd attended a supporters' club Christmas function and he'd given a couple of the fans a lift. 'Do you like the leopard skin seats?' he teased. 'I shot 'em myself!'

In the decades that followed Munich, the introductory question in conversation that the widows came to dread was: 'And what does your husband do for a living?' Or if it was mother or father of a dead boy: 'Where does your son work?' Once they had been able to reply: 'Professional footballer.'

Few had experience of the death of loved ones and while these days professional grief counsellors would have been queuing at their doors, the only support then came from their immediate friends and family. The club couldn't, or wouldn't, help either.

After the funerals it became worse. The families, like David Pegg's redoubtable father Bill and Liam Whelan's mother may have been able to hold back their tears at the ceremony, but perhaps they were so numbed they could not react. The depressions came later with the anniversaries of 6 February an annual reminder. Even now, the pain for the Munich families arrives every time they think of that day, a pain they can do nothing about it. Some, however, are determined never to forget.

'We met at fifteen and courted till we were twenty-one and twenty and then got married,' says Jones's widow, June. 'He was a lovely man, kind, honest and a great husband and dad. He liked to go shooting and took his dog Ric. We were only together four-and-a-half years. He went to Manchester United when he was about sixteen, but I didn't take much notice at the time because it was the man I was interested in, not the football. Sometimes I wish he had never played and maybe he would still be with me and the family, the son he knew for two-and-a-half years and the daughter he never knew and his four grandchildren who he would have loved. He only wanted a family and of course to play football but what did football get him? Killed at twenty-four. He had all his life in front of him and never got to live it. I wasn't interested in the football life, all I wanted was him and the children.

'He has two grandsons, Mark who is called after him and Wayne and two granddaughters, Lisa and Laura. I know he would have been so proud of them and he has never had the joy of seeing them grow up. Lynn never knew him and Gary was only two and a half so he doesn't remember him.

'Mark is buried just down the road from where we live and I can visit him when I want which is two or three times a week. We didn't want the life these footballers have today, we would have been happy in our semi in Manchester. I've never been to a football match since, I can't and won't go because it would be Mark and all the ones he played with I would see, not the players of today. I did take my grandsons to Old Trafford and they went out on the pitch and kicked a ball around and met the team who were very nice to them.

'I have a sad day every 6 February and I'm not fit to talk to on that day so I just go to the grave with some flowers and sit there awhile. It has been over forty years but I am not going to forget him.'

Another member of Manchester United's three-strong White Rose platoon had signalled his arrival at Old Trafford with a scoring header from outside the penalty area against Preston North End in his first game for his new club on 7 March 1953. It made Tommy Taylor an instant hero among supporters and management desperate for a traditional centre-forward who could take advantage of the work done by the schemers behind. The following five years, until Munich, would do nothing to dissuade them all that here was a very special talent.

'The most under-rated player of the last fifty years,' is John Doherty's verdict on a man who managed two goals every three matches, with a further sixteen in nineteen games for England. At twenty-six, he was still approaching his peak at the time of Munich.

Taylor had been bought by United from Barnsley for what was then a record fee of £29,999. Busby, allegedly, had not wanted him burdened with a £30,000 price tag, but newspapers being newspapers and not in the business of semantics even in those days, Taylor immediately found himself labelled the first £30,000 footballer. It was said he could head a ball more accurately than many players could kick it. This spectacular talent tended to obscure his other abilities. He could look clumsy on the ball but he possessed fine control and astute distribution. His partnership with Dennis Viollet was devastatingly productive.

His fame soon spread and immediately after the 1957 FA Cup Final, in which he scored United's only goal, Inter Milan made the then astronomical offer of £65,000 for him, an offer Busby didn't even give serious consideration.

He liked his beer, but there was no more dedicated trainer and his genetic gifts allowed him to recover from having both cartilages out of each knee in an era when such an operation amounted to butchery. Built like an Adonis, team-mates would recall the Yorkshireman polishing off a dozen bottles of lager, and then running at three-quarter pace in training next day, the sweat pouring off him until you could fill a cup full of it.

With his curly black hair, winning smile and jaunty self-belief, he also had his share of female fans, one of them at one time being David Pegg's sister, Irene.

'They all, David, Bob [Charlton] and Tommy, went to the dance halls together,' she says. 'I was very keen on Tommy until I realized he was a gobby bugger. Once he went in the local barbers when it was raining and told the man to keep cutting till it stopped. He was so proud of his hair but they cut it so short he wouldn't take his hat off after.'

The arrival of her brother and his two illustrious team-mates for weekends in Highfields was to provide lasting memories, not only for the small mining village, but Irene herself.

'They used to come over in their big cars and play with the local kids,' she says. 'When Bobby came to unveil a plaque to David in Highfields Working Men's Club organized by the Doncaster branch of the MUFC Supporters Club, a lot of the folk who had been around at that time came along and I think Bob enjoyed that. Bob and our David were mates because they came from similar backgrounds, mining and working class. It was the same with Tommy.'

There was little doubt, according to Irene, that David was the apple of many eyes, notably those of their father, Bill.

'You see all those pictures of our David, always with a smile on his face? That was exactly how he was. He was just a genuinely nice lad. I can remember going to Old Trafford when our David was playing and we used to get there so late we'd be in part of ground where you could only see people's legs going past. We were miners' kids and lived in a mining village and we were just ordinary kids. Our David was the oldest and went to Highfields primary, infant juniors and seniors which all shared the same quadrangle. When I was at school I used to threaten kids and say: "If you don't stop that I'll get my big brother on you." And my big brother would say: "Stop saying that cos your big brother's not fighting for you or anyone else." He was always busy, he was the busy one in the family. Where we lived in Highfields we were in blocks of six, with a ginnel [passageway] in between that was the width of the house. Like David Beckham's mum says of her lad, David would always be kicking a ball against the wall. There's no doubt that David was the light of our dad's eye.'

Pegg was fifteen when he left Highfields and he needed special dispensation to leave school early. Bill Pegg agreed with Busby that his son would serve an apprenticeship, but in the end football took over.

'He went to a joiners, where the men used to feed him up because he was so little,' says Irene. 'But he never lasted there. We didn't have a telephone so when he was in Manchester he would send us cards or ring my sister Doreen at the solicitors where she worked.

'Most weeks he came home with his shirts for ironing by Mum. "No one like my mum can iron shirts," he would say. There's a famous picture of David in his digs at Mrs Watson's doing the dishes. He didn't do the dishes, he didn't do anything about the house. I think he told the photographer: "I'll hold the cloth but I'm not using it".'

He took his responsibilities as a Manchester United footballer seriously. As did Taylor, whose family found a guide to public speaking in his Manchester digs when they went to collect his belongings.

'David would often be invited back to school to present cups and to local galas to give speeches and he rehearsed all the speeches and learned how to speak in public. Tommy did the same. David also practised signing autographs. David had a lot of girlfriends, but he was not a committer. He was very good-looking and I had loads of friends who were after him. I sang in a choir, the Wheatsheaf Girls' Choir, and lots of lasses would ask if David was coming.

'Sean, my son, is like our David. A smiler. Mum, who is in a home now, looks at him and he smiles and I think she sees our David.'

Like every other family, the Peggs were traumatized by Munich, the effects hardly helped by the manner in which they were given the news.

'The doorbell rang at 7 am on the day after the crash and it was a policeman,' says Irene. 'He didn't waste words and said straight out: "Tha' David's dead, what dost want doing with t'body?" I will never forget this big man in uniform stood there in the door. He just walked straight in and came out with that and it's exactly what he said. There's no nice way of saying it, I know, but there's nicer ways of saying it.

'That was Friday morning and then all hell broke loose. Mother had the worst time, she was devastated. Dad was strong. "We won't have none of this blubbering," he said on the day of the funeral. Everyone had to have a stiff upper lip. It helped us with being away from Manchester.

'The local newspapers didn't bother us, although one reporter who went to school with me, Peter Whittell, and we are still friends now, parked his bottom on the settee on the day of the crash. I answered the door to him and he said there had been an accident. "We think your David's been involved."

'Had he been driving too fast? We didn't know where he was, we didn't even know he was abroad. Peter Whittell stayed there, although maybe he shouldn't. He told me years after it was his job.

'After he died I thought for a while my mother was going to go mental. There was thousands at the funeral, and all these people in the house that no one knew. Policemen were directing traffic, the road was closed and that's what did Mum in. It was as if the Queen was coming. It were awful. You're there just as a bystander, but he was my brother, not an international footballer.'

Pegg, who was twenty-two at the time of his death, did not leave much in the way of worldly goods.

'Dad and Uncle Frank went to Mrs Watson's in Manchester to fetch his car. Our Sean has his Real Madrid watch and tie. I go to the cemetery every two weeks and on special occasions make sure it's all cleaned up. As for Manchester United, I knew the old school and they are not there any more. A couple of times I've rung and asked for tickets for my grandson.

'Someone still puts flowers on his grave. I know which flowers I put on and there is still someone leaves a flower on it. I'd love to know who it is.

'The grave's in good order and some folk still think the club look after it. There's lots who believe they pay for the flowers on the grave. Maybe it's because they are red and white.'

8

THE KNIGHTS' TALE

'A bunch of bouncing Busby Babes, they deserve to be knighted.' So went the original Manchester United calypso, recorded in 1955 by the Trinidadian actor/singer Edric Connor, with the backing of Ken Jones and His Music. The song is never chanted on the Old Trafford terraces these days, events having conspired to make the sentiments redundant. And in any case the Babes calypso long ago gave way in popularity to more basic contemporary classics such as 'Always look out for Turks wielding knives' (to the tune of *Always Look on the Bright Side of Life* and a reminder to Leeds fans that two of their number were once stabbed to death in Istanbul). But Connor's innocent little ditty did contain an element of foresight. The men most closely associated with the Babes era did eventually hire toppers for the trip to the Palace. Busby's knighthood arrived in 1969 and although Bobby Charlton had to wait

another twenty-five years, the two most high-profile survivors of Munich and the only two whose careers could be
said to have flourished to any great extent following the air
crash, certainly deserved the recognition. Busby, even then,
had already been regarded as one of British football's
greatest managers, Charlton as one of its greatest players
and, later, a much-loved, globe-trotting ambassador for the
game.

When Manchester United did finally win the European
Cup, ten years after Munich on a desperately hot and
humid 29 May night in London, they had come to the end
of a long and painful journey. 'Busby ends his quest for the
Holy Grail' said the large headline in the *Manchester
Evening News* and for once the hyperbole and poetic
licence was justified, for it had been an Arthurian quest of
fabulous proportions which had lasted over sixteen years.
When the whistle finally blew at Wembley to end a techni-
cally mediocre match distinguished by the drama of extra-
time and two symbolic goals from Charlton himself, Busby
walked on to the field and headed straight for his captain.
Their embrace told everything of the dramas they had
shared, of the suffering, the frustration and the undoubted
relief of that final fulfilment.

That European Cup victory came not a moment too
soon. Charlton, who was thirty-one by then and Busby,
who was close to sixty and one year away from his first
retirement, would never have got another chance, nor a

better one. The team that won in 1968, as was soon to be proven, was on its last legs and it was to be another thirty-one years before United got hands on the trophy again. But if they were to fulfil what they regarded as their destiny in the 1967–68 European Cup campaign, they could not have been granted a better winning hand.

The metaphorical Rubicon had been crossed by a vibrant Celtic side coached by Busby's fellow Scot Jock Stein twelve months earlier, so the beckoning precedent was there. The 1968 final was also scheduled fortuitously for Wembley, a second home for the likes of Charlton and the gamecock wing-half Nobby Stiles. United also had George Best and Denis Law – although the Scot did not play in the final – in their pomp and the support, arguably for the last time, of a large part of the nation. The early rounds of the tournament had also favoured them with modest opposition. First up were Hibernian of Malta, who were coached by a Valetta priest. They farcically mislaid one of their players when he became lost while buying an ice cream in London en route to Manchester. The Maltese were duly dispatched 4–0 at Old Trafford, but there was a potent clue that time was running out for Busby and his ageing team when they were held 0–0 in the return.

A ruthless FC Sarajevo team were subdued in the next round and the first real scare came in the quarter-final, although not from the opposition. Gornik Zabrze of Poland had knocked out Celtic, and although United took a healthy 2–0 lead to Poland the snow that fell steadily throughout the match brought back some disconcerting memories. In the end, United lost 1–0 and were through to their fourth European Cup semi-final where an equally long-toothed Real Madrid side – Francisco Gento the scourge of United so often in the past was by then thirty-five – contrived to throw away a 3–2 aggregate lead, with United's two vital second-half goals coming from their defenders, David Sadler and Bill Foulkes. It was the first time anyone could ever recall the centre-half venturing past the halfway line.

The Portuguese champions, Benfica, were United's final opponents at Wembley and again the omens were good. They had dismantled the same opposition 5–1 in Lisbon's Stadium of Light in 1966 and Stiles, as he had demonstrated in the World Cup semi-final against Portugal in the same year, seemed to have the number of the Benfica danger man, Eusebio.

Charlton had also enjoyed one of his best games for England against the Portuguese in 1966, scoring the two goals that took England into the final. Amazing as it may seem now in these days of niggardly professionalism, two of the Portuguese players shook Charlton's hand as he made his way back, in that characteristic arm-swinging manner, to the centre circle.

Even so, United still made heavy work of Benfica two years later. Charlton's first goal on fifty-three minutes should have sufficed, but they conceded a needless equalizer when the gangling centre-forward Jose Torres, engaged in an often-comical duel with the equally maladroit Foulkes, nodded down a cross for Jaime Graca to lash past Alex Stepney. The goalkeeper's stupendous stop from Eusebio close to full-time had, like most great saves, an element of fortune about it and the match-winner, in the end, turned out to be the unsung and unheralded left wing John Aston, who ran the Portuguese ragged in extra-time. United had reached the promised land.

After Wembley 1968, the only question left was, where now? Sir Galahad had a World Cup winner's medal, was Footballer of the Year and arguably the most instantly recognizable Englishman on the planet. King Arthur had his Holy Grail, a knighthood, the promise of some sort of sinecure at Old Trafford when he did step down and a grown-up family. His son, Sandy, has few doubts, either, that his father was losing his appetite for the day-to-day demands of football management.

'Dad, like all good managers had always had a very clear vision of what was good for the club. But sentiment came in, in 1968, with that ageing team. He knew in his heart of hearts that it was time to start dismantling it and start building again. But at his stage of life, sixty, he simply hadn't the heart or ruthlessness to ship Bobby and Bill Foulkes out to other clubs.

'George [Best] was always complaining that he was

carrying an ageing team. His decision to retire was because he no longer had the heart or ruthlessness to do what was needed to be done.'

Much has been written about Busby's managerial skills; his quiet, persuasive charm, organization, and his occasional ruthlessness. The image is very often that of a kindly grand-father figure who preferred his assistant, Jimmy Murphy, to play the bad cop. The truth is that Busby used this image in public but in private he could be as ruthless as any and it would be naïve to believe that any manager without some degree of steel could win as much in the cut-throat world of football. Unlike many former players turned coaches, he was not an advocate of improved player power with better con-tracts and wages, although he did develop a habit of reward-ing the smokers in his side with a Rothmans after every match, win, lose or draw. He tolerated the wayward genius of George Best, but he punished other players harshly, such as Johnny Morris, Charlie Mitten and Dennis Viollet, for stepping out of line and undermining his authority.

Busby certainly knew the right buttons to press on a player. When the Old Trafford crowd, misled by the Irishman's languid style, began to get on his back, Liam Whelan had asked Busby to leave him out of the team because 'they are all having a go at me'. Busby's reply was: 'Worry when I have a go at you, son.'

According to Harry Gregg: 'There was something about him. It was not fear, it was more like a headmaster, a priest, a minister. I only heard him raise his voice twice and it was to the same person. He called Bill Foulkes a tramp. "How I ever signed you. Shut up. How I made you captain, I'll never know. You're a tramp." The same thing happened at West Ham in the same year.

'There was this finger-pointing thing and Bill was the worst at it. He never opened his mouth because he had nothing to say, but he would be finger pointing and the crowd would shout: "Good old Cowboy". The lads hated it.' Busby's injuries, which had left him in constant pain, meant he could never return to the hands-on approach of a tracksuited manager. The mental scars remained hidden. 'He never, ever, spoke about Munich,' says Sandy.

It is no secret that during his long convalescence in hospital in Germany, Busby had seriously thought of giving up. As he drifted in and out of consciousness he asked continually about 'the boys'. His wife Jean, daughter Sheena and Sandy kept the truth away from him until Jean Busby finally grasped the nettle.

'Dad began to go through the names one by one,' says Sandy. 'When he got to the name of a player, Mum either shook her head, or nodded.'

It was then, as Busby admitted later that 'I felt like dying. I felt that, in a way, I might have been responsible. That I shouldn't have allowed us to go the third time. What was so special about me that I'd survived? I was absolutely determined that I'd have nothing more to do with football.'

After he hobbled on crutches out of hospital in Munich, United sent the Busbys to Interlaken, in Switzerland, for an extended period of convalescence and it was there that Jean said casually one evening, 'You know, Matt, the lads would have wanted you to carry on.' The melancholic spell was broken. He returned by rail and sea to arrive on 18 April, seventy-one days after the crash. In his absence, United had struggled to the FA Cup Final, where they played their old rivals Nat Lofthouse and Bolton Wanderers.

Busby arrived on crutches, Charlton hit a post, but Lofthouse bundled Gregg over the line, United lost 2–0 and the great adventure was over. Even so, there had been hope in the symbolic appearance of Busby, the phoenix emblazoned on the United jerseys and the sighting of the great white hope, Charlton.

The celebrated journalist and chatshow host Michael Parkinson insists to this day that the United team that reached Wembley in May, 1958, has never been accorded the recognition it deserves for what had been a rare feat of arms by a rag-tag outfit of youngsters from the reserves and bought-in veterans. Nor has Jimmy Murphy been granted the status he merits at Old Trafford.

Charlton certainly has few doubts, crediting the Welshman, to the occasionally pointed exclusion of Busby, for 'everything I have achieved in football'.

When he scored what is seen as the defining, great Charlton goal against Mexico in 1966, running from deep within his own half, swerving, feinting and finally delivering an unstoppable shot right of the goalkeeper, the credit went to Murphy. 'It's the old Jimmy Murphy in me,' said Charlton. 'Don't aim at a specific part of the goal, just get it on target.' It was an admission that came as a shock to those of us who were convinced that everything Charlton did on a football field was informed by studied deliberation, but the message was clear: all those hours with Murphy on the training paddock, combined with a glorious, innate talent, had produced a very special footballer.

'Jimmy would take broken-hearted players and spin them a fairy story,' says Harry Gregg. 'He was certainly the making of Charlton. He got him to cut out the glory balls early on in his career, and bollocked him for attempting the difficult when something simpler was more productive and the work he did with all the kids was phenomenal.

'Jimmy would cry with you, sing with you, a lovable, outlandish, crazy Welshman with an Irish name. If Matt hadn't come back from Munich Jimmy would have started the Third World War; every player in the club would have been an alcoholic and directors would not have been allowed in the boardroom. He was anti-establishment up to here.'

Like the pre-Munich Busby, Murphy went to work in a baggy tracksuit tucked into a pair of woollen socks and favoured exciting attacking play, but within the framework of an uncomplicated method.

'Jimmy was a hard taskmaster, a hard taskmaster with brains,' says John Doherty. 'He never asked people to do what they were not capable of. I was a good player, a class player but I was never a kicker so he never asked me to do that. Wilf McGuinness, to me, was just a kicker, that's all he could do. He'd say to Bill Foulkes: "There's the stand, Bill, kick it in there, don't try and pull it down and do anything fancy."'

It is unarguable that of all the recruits he was to bring into Old Trafford over the three decades he was in charge there, Busby's most significant signing was that of his assistant. Busby had certainly known Murphy before the famous incident at a transit camp in Bari, Northern Italy towards the end of the war when he heard the Welshman give a riveting team talk to a spellbound group of football-playing soldiers. In United folklore this is often given the same significance as Rogers meeting Hammerstein or Morecambe meeting Wise, but the two men had certainly come across each other before Bari. Murphy had won fifteen caps for Wales and had played against Busby at club level in the late Thirties, the Welshman as a wing-half for Swindon and the Scot at Liverpool.

Like most flourishing double acts in every walk of life the two Celts had virtually nothing in common apart from football, a belief that the game belonged to the young, a strict Catholic upbringing in straitened circumstances and a fondness for Scotch whisky.

The fiery, fast-talking Murphy was the antithesis of Busby and far happier on the training ground than chatting to the press or tending to administrative duties.

As well as the Babes, he had notable success with the Welsh national side leading a squad distinguished by *Il Gigante Buono*, John Charles, his brother Mel and Ivor Allchurch to the 1958 World Cup finals. 'Jimmy was a tremendous character and he brought the best out of the players,' says the spring-heeled winger of that team, Cliff Jones. 'He had magnificent enthusiasm and commitment, and that rubbed off on the players.'

His methods were unique. 'Jimmy would spit and snarl at you but his football brain was something else,' says Albert Scanlon. 'In the Fifties we were drawn with Walthamstow Avenue in the Youth Cup and Jimmy had us all in a circle with Bert Whalley. "The FA have started a Youth Cup and we are going to win it. Isn't that right, Bert?" And Bert would say "Yes" right back. They were like Laurel and Hardy.

'The first game was against Leeds, who had Jack Charlton at centre-half and we beat them 4–0. We made changes for the second match and there was 10,000 at The Cliff. We beat Nantwich 23–0, murdered them 23–0 . . . and Jimmy signed their goalkeeper so he wouldn't go out of the game.

'He had no intention of playing him, but he didn't want him disheartened and despondent. Who would do that? He told the kid: "You can't be that bad because we signed you." For the third game, they brought Eddie Colman in and then flew in a lad in from Dublin, Tommy Hamilton. We beat Bury, we beat Barnsley 3–1 in a game I scored off my shin and I remember after Jack Rowley called me a jammy bleeder. We got drawn away against Brentford in the semi-final – Wolves had got Huntley and Palmers Biscuit Works, believe it or not.'

Before the Brentford match Murphy delivered one of his team talks. 'There was a guy who wrote about youth football in the *Mirror* and this article stuck in Murphy's craw,' adds Scanlon. 'It was something on the lines of Brentford being the best youth team he had ever seen. We went down to London, and stayed in the Lancaster Court and we went out to see *Kismet* with David Hughes and Sally Ann Howes. Unknown to us they also brought our parents down, though they stayed in a different hotel.

'The lads were getting lined up in the dressing room and there was Jimmy, Bert and Arthur Powell, who was a groundsman, but also a fully qualified St John's Ambulanceman. He had salts and all that in his bag as well as three or four packets of fags. He was an incessant smoker, and must have got through about a thousand fags during a match.

'Jimmy speaks up: "Got any Cockneys or Londoners?"
'Bert said: "No. John and Duncan are from the Midlands,

Bryce is from Eccles but he's Scots. Paddy and Noel are from Dublin, Eddie, John and Albert from Manchester, Ronnie's from Crewe and David, Doncaster. No, no Cockneys or Londoners."

'Jimmy threw the ball at Ron and said: "Right Ron, let's get out cos I hate these fucking Cockneys. Let's give them a fucking hammering." We finished with nine men and beat them 2–0 and all you could get out of Jimmy was: "What's Evans going to write this week then?"'

Murphy's feat in taking Wales to the 1958 World Cup finals for the only time in their history and where they beat Hungary, only to lose 1–0 to eventual champions Brazil, brought him to the attention of other club sides, keen to harness his obvious coaching abilities. Arsenal had tried to woo him in 1957, as did Juventus, and after the World Cup, a Brazilian official rang the Welshman to offer him what was an unheard of figure of £30,000 to coach there. Murphy turned them all down.

It would be rewarding to believe that this remarkable man's dedication to United was reciprocated, but sadly it was not. After Busby retired, Murphy was given the title of club scout, but then sidelined by a succession of managers who plainly saw him as an anachronism. Eventually, he lost his office and United informed him they would no longer pay for his taxis and phone bills.

'By the time Jimmy died in 1989 he and Matt were strangers,' says Gregg. 'It was heartbreaking. Jimmy never

showed his feelings but it must have come close to breaking him.'

As he had two years earlier in the same arena when England
reached the end of another long and winding road and lifted
the Jules Rimet trophy, Bobby Charlton wept copiously at
the end of the 1968 final, the emotions flooding out of a man
usually noted for his unsmiling, reserved demeanour. Later,
as the United party celebrated long into the night, someone
looked round for the captain, but whether through tiredness
or emotion he had retired to his hotel room long before midnight. The curtains had been drawn again.

It would take a very odd personality not to be changed
by something as traumatic as a plane crash in which a large
number of friends died, and Charlton's metamorphosis was
immediate. The stern, unsmiling manner he adopted after
Munich was the most notable sign that his youth, in a
metaphorical sense, came to an end there. The burdens and
expectations thrust upon him from then on could only be
borne by a powerful and focused personality, but like
many survivors in the public eye, he was wary of how
others would view him.

The first clue that Charlton had settled on the image he
would carry henceforth through life came in hospital in
Munich when he was close to discharge and a return to
England.

'He had asked me to go and look for a coat,' says Sandy Busby. 'I brought one back, a navy blue Italian-style job and Bob took one look at it and said: "Sandy, it's too flash, I can't be seen in that."'

Pre-Munich, Charlton had been one of the boys. Despite a low tolerance for alcohol he enjoyed the occasional drink, usually with his best friend David Pegg, and like every other young player at Old Trafford – Duncan Edwards included – had flirted with smoking. He was also an enthusiastic, but hopelessly unskilled, poker player on United away trips.

He idolized Pegg and it was the young Yorkshireman who had taken Charlton under his wing when he first arrived from the North-East. Their shared background helped an unlikely friendship along. Pegg was a handsome smiling lad of twenty-two with film-star looks and a ready smile, Charlton shy and unprepossessing. After Pegg bought his first car, a light-blue Vauxhall Victor, Charlton did likewise. His was dark blue and Tommy Taylor followed suit with a red one and the three of them – in three separate cars – would motor in convoy across to Bill and Jessie Pegg's home in Highfields, travelling in those pre-M62 days over the Howden and Thurlstone moors and parking line abreast in the street, much to the astonishment of the neighbours.

Once, on the border between Lancashire and Yorkshire, a policeman flagged Pegg down and asked him 'if you've got a pilot's licence for this thing'.

'Our David took Bob under his wing,' says Pegg's sister Irene. 'Bob was shy and my dad and his brother taught them both how to fish on the Trent. They would go to sleep on the bank. Tommy was lovely and Bob was a smashing lad. I think he had problems with George Best later because of the examples of David, Liam Whelan and the others.'

According to Mrs Beevers, who bears a remarkable resemblance to her brother, Charlton may have had other problems: 'He keeps his distance from me now and Norma, his wife, told me he has difficulty looking at me. She says Bob can hear David in my laugh. It's the same with Harry Gregg, but why they should feel guilty is beyond me. Having said that, me and my sister also had difficulties. We felt David had been the chosen one.'

It was in America, the land that demands that every facet of the human psyche is carefully defined, that the phrase 'survivor guilt' first originated.

Used to describe a condition afflicting survivors of major disasters, it manifests itself in a constant questioning of why they survived when others did not.

Harry Gregg, who emerged physically unscathed from the wreckage at Reim Airport and went on to a fine career with Manchester United and Northern Ireland, has no problems in admitting that he suffered survivor guilt for close to forty years after the crash. 'I couldn't look them in the eyes,' he says.

The Munich Memorial Service at Manchester Cathedral

in 1998 and the subsequent match on the anniversary against Bolton Wanderers, finally exorcised Gregg's ghosts. He met Roger Byrne Jnr, by then almost forty, at the service but it was when Joy Byrne took the big Irishman in her arms and said: 'Harry Gregg, why have you been torturing yourself for these forty years?' that the guilt was washed away and he is able to say now: 'That was when I was finally able to confront my demons.'

According to psychologists, there is another prime symptom of survivor guilt: an increased desire to achieve. Charlton may have problems still in looking David Pegg's sister in the eye, but nor can anyone argue about the level of his achievements.

Charlton had been a target for a dozen leading clubs from the age of thirteen with all sorts of inducements being thrown at his mother, Cissie, who said: 'I'd be cleaning the fireplace in the morning and I'd look round and there'd be another one standing behind me. There were times when we had one in the front room and one in the kitchen. They were offering us the world. One fellow offered £800. Another said he'd double whatever was the highest offer we'd had. He didn't even ask what it was.'

Like Duncan Edwards, Charlton by rights should have gone to his local club. His uncle was the swashbuckling Newcastle and England striker Jackie Milburn and he would go to St James' Park in anticipation of seeing the great players from other famous clubs. His favourite was

Stanley Matthews, from whom he learned the importance of speed off the mark.

It was the late 1940s and Matthews was at his peak. Charlton recalled: 'You could stand on the cinders in front of the terracing. The men used to pass you down over their heads. Stan was magic. We all like dribblers and he was the wizard. I would study him and think: "What makes him better than anybody else?" My uncles said: "Just watch his first ten yards."'

Charlton had been blessed with fast-twitch fibres, but worked hard on his sprinting with his grandfather, who had trained professional sprinters. Later, at the peak of his game, there was no one quicker over those first ten yards. He was fifteen and fresh out of school when he decided to join Manchester United, Cissie having been charmed by the winning combination of Busby and Jimmy Murphy on a visit to Ashington.

Charlton's exploits are well documented and do not need repeating here. In his early days he played on the left wing, occasionally at inside-forward, but it was in the deep-lying centre-forward role, the equivalent of today's central attacking midfielder, that he is best remembered, along with his explosive shooting – 245 goals in 751 games for United – astute passing and a formidable workrate.

By 1971, however, it was clear that the star was on the wane. He had never played for England again after being controversially substituted in the 1970 World Cup quarter-final against Germany in Leon and twelve months later the pace had gone, along with most of the hair, and he was thirty-four years old. The then United manager Tommy Docherty faced a tough choice, and one that Busby had been unwilling to confront.

'I was thinking that I'd have to make the decision and didn't want to do it,' says Docherty. 'There would have been a public outcry. But he came to see me and said he was thinking about retiring. I breathed a huge sigh of relief. I'm glad he made the decision and not me.'

There were less gilded arenas. He tried management with Preston – for whom he turned out as a player in 1974, the year he was awarded the CBE – and later became a director at Wigan Athletic, both with a depressing lack of success. However, he did return to United, as a member of the football board in 1994, the year he was knighted.

Charlton's new status, however, was to cause inevitable tensions between him and some of the Munich survivors, and vice versa, as he sought to maintain a balancing act between duty to club and his friendship with former team-mates.

This was to come to a head at the Champions' League Final of 1997 when an inspired UEFA invited all the survivors back to Munich for the match between Borussia Dortmund and Juventus. The grizzled veterans obligingly posed for photographs and gave a press conference where Foulkes once again gave his version of events on the airfield, only to be contradicted by Gregg at the other end of the table. The Irishman found it hard to stay quiet, too, when Charlton announced that 'Every day of my life I think of the crash and the lads who died there.'

Gregg says: 'Aye, I thought "If that's what you believe then why the fuck have you done nothing for some of the others all this time?"'

9

OUT OF SIGHT, OUT OF MIND

Albert Scanlon had suggested Pendleton Church as a rendezvous, although its spire, from a distance, was lost in the grey surrounds of urban Salford and far more difficult to find than his home, which turned out to be less than a mile away. The portly, bespectacled figure was there on time all right, waiting patiently in the overgrown graveyard and muffled by cap and coat against the wintry rigours of the dirty old town. He did not look round as I approached and the only plausible explanation for this curious, Le Carré-esque behaviour was to come later from Harry Gregg: 'That's Albert,' said Scanlon's lifelong friend with an understanding smile. 'That *is* Albert.'

At Old Trafford they knew him as Joe Friday, the laconic, white-coated police lieutenant from *Dragnet*, the American TV series which went out two or three times a week on Associated Television, usually sandwiched between *This Week* and *Highway Patrol*. Scanlon favoured a white raincoat, too, although he disputes the source of his nickname: 'It was because I was always around whenever something was going off.'

Streetwise, but open and magnanimous, Scanlon must have had as many close shaves down the years as his fictional alter ego. According to Gregg, on arrival on foreign soil with United, Scanlon would immediately browse through the local phone directory, pick out what appeared to be an English surname and phone them, getting 'a guide for a good night out – and no need to learn the lingo'. On one tour of America in the Fifties he persuaded the coach driver to drop him off in New York city and spent a night in Harlem, turning up later, unharmed and unabashed, at the team hotel.

'When I had the hotel in Portstewart he would come across and everyone loved him,' says Gregg. 'Once when he was over he fancied a night out on his own so I left him in Coleraine, which is a very big town, and he found his way back home to Portstewart. Yes, Albert was always around. When we went to America it was on the old *Queen Mary* and I am lying on my bunk one night when these bouncers turn up and say: "Where's the party? Albert invited us." He is so laid back he would fall over. A year after the crash we flew to Rotterdam to play Feyenoord about the time Scanny had been picked for England B.

It was the first flight after Munich for a lot of them. Ian Greaves cried off and Foulkes was in a bad way going over. We went by coach from Leicester to Heathrow and flew from there. We landed in Rotterdam and I was rooming with Scanny. Tricky Viollet, of course, had imported his own bird from England.

'I never drank, but we were in a nightclub in Rotterdam and the thing with Matt Busby was that if the lads were in a club and he was there they would buy him a drink and then get the hell out of there, and vice versa. So that's what we did. But I remember outside this nightclub holding Scanny upright and the Boss came out and said to me: "Good night Big Fella." Albert was spewing all round him. He is getting up at 7 am that morning to go and play for England and the last I saw of him he was lying stretched out on his bed, like a corpse, and with a bunch of lilies in his hand. Next morning when I got up he was gone, back to England. He was man of the match at Highbury. That's Albert.'

John Doherty was in the same United party for the Feyenoord match and he remembers things slightly differently: 'After the game we were supplied with tickets for drinks and Greggy comes up to me and says: "Don't, whatever you do, give Scanlon any."

"Right Harry."

'Albert was rooming with Harry and when I went up to the room later they were having a right row. Greggy had him dangling outside the window saying: "The little bastard's been smoking in the room again."'

Home for Albert Scanlon today is just off Seedley Road, close by Salford rugby league ground, the city's other Red Devils, and within a mile of Weaste cemetery where Eddie Colman lies. I knew he had no telephone because to contact him you have to call a friend between 10 and 11 am and then ring the same number again the following day when the message had been passed on.

'One of his daughters put a block on his phone,' explains Gregg. It turned out there was no electricity, either, until he put 50p in the meter and the carton of milk for our tea, in the absence of a refrigerator, was kept in a cupboard below a sink piled high with unwashed crockery. An even larger stack of nylon shirts lay atop an ancient ironing board and the council house smelled of damp and cigarette smoke.

'I must give these bleedin' things up,' spluttered Scanlon without conviction between alarming coughing fits. In the middle of this chaos stood a splendid, and almost new, wide-screen television, purchased, presumably, with part of his payment from the Munich testimonial fund in 1998. Some of the other proceeds, according to Gregg, went to the Omagh bomb appeal and to the family of the Coventry City steward crushed by a reversing coach, both events in the same year. 'Albert has always been a giver, never a taker,' says Gregg.

Scanlon lives alone, although he has had a relationship with the same woman for seventeen years and there are two former wives somewhere – and seven children. One boy is in his fifties and a policeman in Liverpool. Scanlon hasn't seen him since he was nine and 'there's another daughter in Los Angeles or somewhere'. The former Manchester United winger's life seems to have come full circle since his birth in St Mary's baby hospital in the elemental Manchester suburb of Hulme in November 1935. More than most, he has come to realize that all glory is fleeting.

Like many other former famous footballers he seems to be simply a relic of a lost era now, remembered and indulged when the anniversaries – particularly that of 6 February 1958 – come round, but no longer a part of the game that made his name. 'I get by,' he says. 'But people tend to think that if you have won a championship or the Cup that's enough.'

Scanlon's grandmother brought him up in Medlock Street in Hulme, close by the gasworks in a house with two bedrooms shared by fifteen others, including the four brothers and seven sisters of his father. Hulme, once known as Little Ireland, is only a mile from the splendours of Manchester's Town Hall and Central Library, but in the Thirties and Forties had changed little from Victorian days when it was considered one of the worst slums in Europe, a maze of aged factories and workshops, terraced houses, cobbled streets and back alleys.

'I went to junior school at St Mary's, but ran out because it was all teaching by nuns. There was a huge schoolyard and iron railings separating the girls from the boys. I was 4 ft 6 in and a right weed at the age of ten when Bill Grundy, the teacher at St Wilfred's Juniors, got me started playing football. Whole classes would all play together.'

Scanlon's playing apprenticeship was to mirror that of virtually every other working-class youngster growing up in the Forties and Fifties.

He would go to matches with his kit folded and ironed and placed in a shoe box. On one 'field' he played on in Hulme at one end there was a bombed fire station, at the other a bombed swimming baths and a huge concrete shed on one side and on the other they were busy building corporation flats.

'The lads' clubs organized leagues, Under-15s, B team and A team and you followed them up. We were undefeated for five years. As a kid I supported City, and Hulme was City territory. Maine Road was the only ground we ever went to. Wednesdays and Saturdays we were at Maine Road.

'We laughed at United. I can recall their first trophy win after the war. They beat Accrington Stanley 4–1 in the Lancashire Cup and there was Johnny Carey stood on the steps at Maine Road with this little trophy and no-one was really bothered cos it was United. But I was. Carey had come to our school once and he went through the usual routine of asking us all what we wanted to do when we grew up. I piped up: "I want to play for United" and they all laughed, Carey included. But I did in the end. Within a few years I was laying out Carey's kit in the first-team dressing room.

'One day I was playing cricket on this spare bit of ground near home and I was backstump because I was the only one who could catch a corkie ball. Anyway, this bloke rolled up in a Homburg coat and scarf and said: "I'm looking for Albert Scanlon." It turned out it was Mr Whetton, who was manager of Manchester Boys. In the end thirty of us walked with that fellah down Stretford Road to get my birth certificate. I was picked for Manchester Boys and we lost 2–1 to Swansea who had Mel Charles and Cliff Jones playing for them. A complete forward line signed for United from that boys' team. Colin Booth, who was captain, missed out – he signed for Wolves.'

One afternoon, towards the end of another boys' game at the end of 1950 Scanlon noticed 'another fellah sat in an overcoat watching us. At the end he said: "I've come to ask you a question: Would you like to sign for Manchester United? I am going to tell you the same as we tell everyone else. We think we can make a footballer out of you, but we are not going to promise anything. What do you say, here and now?" I said "Yes".

'It was Jimmy Murphy and that was the last I saw of him till the following April when I went to Old Trafford. I signed schoolboy forms in 1950, one of the first Busby Babes and one of the lucky ones as it turned out. There was up to 450 kids a week playing trials. The next week they had all gone, to be replaced by others. You'd never see most of them again.'

Scanlon went down to Old Trafford on a Sunday morning at Easter, where he was introduced to Tom Curry and Busby, after the manager arrived back from Mass. He signed the appropriate forms, and was told they wanted him there the next Tuesday. Then, as he recalls, 'they gave me a brush'.

The apprenticeship was long and hard.

'We had beautiful summers then, everything seemed brighter and sunnier, but they kept you at it at United; they really made you sweat, Murphy in particular. He'd have had you training twenty-four hours a day if he could. The others had their own little ways, too. Early on, Bert Whalley told me to go and get my boots and head over to Littleton Road playing fields where I would find the Colts. I had growing pains in my back and said I couldn't play that day, but all Bert said was: "Do as you are told." So I carry my boots over Trafford Bridge, all the way to Littleton Road in Lower Kersal, bloody miles. I was knackered. A few years later, I asked Bert: "Why did you send me all that bleeding way, all the way across Manchester and Salford, when I couldn't play?" And Bert said: "To show you who's boss."

'In the dressing room you had to be there for nine, then go and get all the kit. There were no tracksuits. We would sweep the first-team dressing room and then we'd have to mop it. There was one big bath, which we would drain while I was mopping the toilets and dressing room. When it was empty I would climb inside the big bath and clean that and hose it down. I would then go in the second-team dressing room and do exactly the same thing.

'They always fed you and a little old lady up Railway Road used to do our dinners, then it was back to work when Bill would say: "Go and do the gym." That was horrendous. There were old mats, a medicine ball, a punch bag and a couple of weights. It was covered in dust and we'd have to mop it, taking about two hours, then Bill says: "Go and dubbin the boots."'

In that first season, between sweeping the ground and cleaning boots Scanlon and his fellow aspirants would sample the delights of competition such as the Eccles League. One match venue was a pig farm at Burnage on the outskirts of Stockport. 'The smell was bloody awful,' he says.

The young United players travelled everywhere by corporation bus. 'We would meet on the left-hand side of the door at the Grand Hotel, on the right of the door would be the Colts. Round the corner there was a coach laid on for the A team with a mixture of full-time pros, semi-pros and amateurs. They got ten bob, we got half a crown. In those days the players didn't train at Old Trafford, but usually at the University Ground in Wythenshawe. They never gave you a ball until the end of the third week, although all that changed after the Hungarians had been.

'The Busby Babes started with the youth team, but Tommy McNulty, Roger Byrne, Don Gibson, who was later to marry Matt's daughter Sheena, Jeff Whitefoot, Cliff Birkett, Brian Birch, Ernie Bond, Frank Clemson, Tommy Ritchie and Ray Hampson were all under twenty.'

By the time of Munich, Scanlon appeared to be close to establishing himself in the United first team. A winger with directness, pace and a fierce shot, but little finesse – 'Albert didn't have a football brain in his head', according to John Doherty – he had been chosen ahead of Pegg for the two league games, against Bolton Wanderers and Arsenal, that preceded the trip to Belgrade. Pegg had taken the decision philosophically, vowing that, 'I will just have to try harder and get my place back' but Scanlon's performance in the 5–4 defeat of Arsenal at Highbury four days before the flight to Belgrade made it certain that he would have a tough job. Scanlon had run the London side's defence ragged and Busby chose the Mancunian, rather than the Yorkshireman, for the European Cup tie.

When the German rescuers found Scanlon unconscious in the snow at Munich they gave him up for dead and left him victims who looked more likely to survive. In fact, although he suffered a fractured skull, Scanlon was on his way back to Manchester from Rechts der Isar hospital within a month. Unlike many of the other players, too, he had seen death at close quarters before, on Boxing Day in 1947, when a friend of his in Hulme borrowed his dad's car and was involved in a massive pile-up on Princess Road. Four were killed and three injured, Scanlon included.

It was this, plus his phlegmatic nature, that undoubtedly helped him back to mental and physical fitness, the United first team and something close to normality, although he knew at once that life could never be the same again. Something more than lives had been extinguished in Germany.

When he arrived back from Munich the taxi driver he had flagged down at Manchester's Victoria Station informed the player that he could have the use of the vehicle,. free of charge, any time he needed it, an act of charity that characterized the people of the city in the wake of Munich; the Samaritan in a black cab was not even a football fan. Albert returned to football, but within a month a club representative took him to one side at Old Trafford and told him United were not prepared to pay for the taxi any more and that he would have to stop using it. United had somehow convinced themselves that they were the benefactors.

Scanlon gave the only reply possible under the circumstances: 'The club has sod all to do with it.'

His conviction that Manchester United did themselves less than justice post-Munich was strengthened when Busby began to unload some of the surviving players in a fashion whose brutality stunned them. He did retain Viollet – at least for a time – Charlton and Foulkes, but Kenny Morgans and Scanlon were moved on without ceremony within a season. Blanchflower and Berry never played again because of the injuries sustained at Munich and it left all of them deeply embittered.

'Jackie Blanchflower and Johnny Berry found life very hard after Munich and I was very disappointed with United,' says Scanlon. 'At least I played forty games for them after the crash. I played half the next season, we got knocked out of the Cup by Norwich and Matt told me he was putting Bobby Charlton in for the next friendly against City which United won 3–1. Matt basically cut us off and I thought he was getting rid of what was left from Munich. Tricky Viollet did a great job for the club, but Matt eventually sold him to Stoke City and he never got a benefit.

'To my mind, Munich killed not only a lot of the players who were on that flight, but some of the survivors, too, and all the young players who had to come in a year or two too early. They were never the same. Things changed for all time at Munich and United didn't come up to par. The two men I blame for it are dead now and that's Busby and

Louis Edwards, who was made chairman just after the crash. They make a show of '58 when it suits them.

'When I went to Newcastle Matt made a promise and never kept it. He told me that financially I would be all right [according to Gregg, Busby had made a similar promise to Morgans when the winger was sold on to his home-town club Swansea]. Matt met me at the Midland Hotel at 11 o'clock at night, and drove me to the Queens. He told me it was best I had a break and left Manchester. "Don't worry, I'll fix all the financial things for you." Five years later I saw him outside the ground and he didn't want to know me.'

At Scanlon's new club, Newcastle United, Scanlon came across an old adversary, the Scottish wild man and club captain, Jimmy Scoular. Their first meeting as team-mates hardly augured well for an enduring friendship.

'The first day at Newcastle Jimmy Scoular had me against the wall: "Don't bring your high-fallutin' Manchester United ways here," he said. What a character he was. Every Friday he would go to Gateshead for the football and every Friday night, nine times out of ten his missus would get a knock on the door and a police constable is there saying: "He's done it again, Mrs Scoular." There's a big island on the Newcastle to Gateshead road and Jimmy just drives straight across it and gets stuck.'

Scanlon spent one season at Newcastle before moving on to Lincoln and then Mansfield, where his career petered out by the age of thirty. After football he worked in a bake-house in Mansfield, then for the tractor makers Massey Ferguson and then went on the docks for sixteen years. He also tried working as a security guard, with twelve-hour shifts. The sole topics of conversation there were football and the Busby Babes.

'The lads I worked with in Civvy Street would always be asking me what was so special about the Busby Babes and I could truthfully tell them that I travelled the world first class in the company of people I wanted to travel with and nothing can take that away. I also got out of the aircraft alive and I am alive today, which is more than you can say for a lot of the others. As for United, they don't bother me now. Ken Merritt and Ken Ramsden give me the time of day, so does the ticket office manager, but 90 per cent, all the young kids, they don't know you. They have never really done 'owt for me. The public paid at the Munich tes-timonial match in 1998, people coming through the gate. They paid Eric Cantona because they said he would put bums on seats, but they could have hung Duncan's shirt on the halfway line and still have filled Old Trafford.

'The ordinary man in the street thinks the club gave us loads of money. I got £260 off the Lord Mayor's fund and there was thousands in that. I have been invited back twice to Old Trafford and I watch certain people go in, the hangers-on, for nowt. If I go to the players' entrance or directors' entrance someone would stop me; people like

Foulkesy walk straight in. Kenny Morgans and me sit in the stand. They think it's enough if you have won things with them, but it's not enough when eight players have lost their lives and families have been destroyed and people thrown out on the street. People had to start again after Munich, people like Mrs Jones, and Mrs Bent.

'Marion Bent didn't want to come into the church for the memorial service in 1998, she didn't think she belonged there even though she was left with a young son and on her own when Geoff died. It was only Greggy who got her in. She thought she was out of place and nobody had spoken to her.

'Two years ago I took a shirt down for charity and they told me they don't sign them now. They will take the shirt off you, then give you another back with one signature, but they can't guarantee it's David Beckham's. People do remember you sometimes. I get stuff shoved through the door, a cutting from *Charles Buchan's Football Monthly* with a piece about me and other notes saying: "I found this and I found that." It's nice when someone remembers you.'

Those sentiments would certainly be echoed by some of the other survivors. Jackie Blanchflower began, tentatively, to write his life story in the early Nineties. He managed only two or three chapters and the book was never published, although his son, Andrew, still has the unfinished manuscript and some tapes containing his father's random thoughts. The book was to open with the author lying, severely injured, in the snow at Munich airfield pinned to his seat by the body of Roger Byrne. In between scanning the airfield for rescue, Blanchflower watched the second hand of his captain's wrist watch ticking away, the machinery still functioning while the pulse beneath was stilled. He had little doubt that, when writing his autobiography, the most dramatic and readable aspects of his life began in a pulverized aircraft at Munich.

Blanchflower survived, but like Johnny Berry, at a fearful cost. Such were the players' travails over the following years that Laurie, one of his two daughters, can wonder now: 'Were the ones that died the ones that got away with it?'

It was Gregg who found Blanchflower in the wreckage, his right arm badly broken and almost severed and his pelvis smashed. Crucially, he also suffered grievous renal damage, a factor that would ultimately shorten his life. The other injuries conspired to end his career. At twenty-five, and with his wife Jean pregnant with their first child, Christa, he was an ex-footballer.

Jackie Blanchflower had spent most of his life fighting long odds. Much of his career was spent in the shadow of his more famous brother Danny, who earned undying fame with Tottenham Hotspur and Northern Ireland, and at Old Trafford he found himself in competition with Mark Jones at centre-half. But as a utility player and a man to rely on in any situation, Blanchflower was priceless. He covered in many positions and produced a rousing display of skill and bravery in the 1957 FA Cup Final after Aston Villa's Peter McParland had cynically put goalkeeper Ray Wood out of the game. Such had been Jackie's assuredness in goal that he was even chosen as a goalkeeper on a subsequent tour by Busby and Murphy.

A Northern Ireland schoolboy international, he arrived at Old Trafford at the age of fifteen to earn undying fame as one of the first Babes and by the time he was twenty-two, he had won a League Championship medal in the 1955–56 season. Not that he was totally devoted to football. According to his son, Andrew, 'Dad and Tommy Taylor used to do illegal boxing. Tommy was Dad's trainer and that's how he used to make extra money to send home to his mum in Northern Ireland. Not that he ever made much because he never won. One day he had a bit of a shiner and he told Matt Busby he had walked into a door. Matt asked if the door was from Yorkshire. Tommy used to tell him "Suss out what your opponent is trying to do, Jack" and dad would come back at the end of the round and say: "I've sussed out what he's trying to do, Tom, he's trying to kill me."'

As with so many others, Blanchflower's life was all about what might have been but for Munich. He played with his brother in a successful Northern Ireland team guided by every Ulsterman's boyhood hero of that era, Peter Doherty, and would undoubtedly have fulfilled a lifetime's dream to have played in Sweden in the summer of 1958 alongside Danny and lifelong friend Gregg. Perhaps he would even have finished up marking Uwe Seeler, Just Fontaine or a seventeen-year-old Brazilian called Pele.

Nine months after the crash a specialist in London told him he couldn't play again. The main concern of the medical team was the kidneys, but his other injuries were to hamper him severely for the rest of his life, too. Like many others in a similar predicament, his first inclination was to look for someone to blame. Then he got bitter.

He bought a newspaper shop, worked for a bookmaker, moved into a pub, became a finance officer, all professions which lasted at the most seven years and all of them brought to an end by the run of bad luck that seemed to haunt him post-Munich. The feeling that the world had deserted him was only exacerbated by Manchester United.

'Jackie told me he never went back to Old Trafford because he was afraid of being turned away,' says Scanlon. 'Once he went down, as we all have done, and tried to get a ticket and the kid in the ticket office, who was probably around eighteen years old, didn't know him. Jackie had wanted two tickets for his doctor, but they turned him away. "That's why I never go back there," Jackie told me.'

Of course Blanchflower did return to Manchester after the crash and within a few months a club representative, the bearer of bad news, told him he would have to vacate the club house, despite Jean's pregnancy. Something, however, must have stirred the conscience of the new chairman, Louis Edwards, for he offered Blanchflower a job with his meat-packaging company . . . loading pies on to lorries.

'Jackie always told me he was living like an animal,' says Harry Gregg. 'I went to see him once and asked him straight: "Have you been trying to play again?" and he replied: "No, I can't." It was heartbreaking.'

One of the recurring themes in researching this book is that while female relatives of the Munich players are almost universally anti-United, their male ones won't have a word said against the club. Jackie's son Andrew, who was forty-three in 2005, can reveal in one breath that the club demanded that his father returned his season ticket 'because he never used it' and other slights 'which I would never tell you or anyone else about' and in the next, he can add: 'At the end of the day my dad played for the team I love and whether they were bad to him or not I still love them. I can't help that.'

Andrew's sister Laurie, like her mother before her, sees things in a different light and while the joint interview, in Laurie's home in Stalybridge, never remotely approached the realms of a family quarrel, it soon became plain that some of their differences will remain irreconcilable.

Laurie says: 'Andrew has been going to Old Trafford since he was four or five, but I don't like football at all.

I don't understand it, and I don't want any connection with it. I have no time at all for Manchester United. The only thing I thank them for is that they wrote and said they would send a representative to my dad's funeral and I thought it would be the toilet cleaner, but it was Alex Ferguson. When I was a child, because my name was Blanchflower, people thought we were brought up with a silver spoon in our mouths. But Dad kept being made redundant. They would be cutting the water off and many times my mum's been hiding behind the settee from the bailiffs. I thought we were playing a game. Twelve months after Munich he was out of work and looking for a house. He wasn't the luckiest of people. Mum used to say he used up all the family's luck surviving Munich. He was always being made redundant.

'The memorial match turned into a pity thing and I don't think they did enough for them in the end. The club could have doubled it, no problems. Mum and Dad didn't have two bob to rub together, I can remember Mum smoking paper. Dad worked for Ronnie Stott, the book-makers, and then bought a sweet shop, Auntie Connie used to run that.

'He bought the pub in 1968 and it was very successful, but then wouldn't you know it, the three-day week came, and then the breathalyser. Then he had a bookies in Todmorden, with a mate, and that fell apart. His mate was taken to court for fiddling tax according to the *Manchester*

Evening News, who put a picture of Danny in the paper and Danny sued them and won £800. Dad never got out of the shadow of Danny. After the bookies he worked in a textile factory in Stalybridge, then Manchester Boys Development Association and got made redundant from there.'

Blanchflower finally got his elusive break in the mid-Eighties. Jean, his wife, was a singer and quite well known on the club scene in the Fifties. At one time she worked with Mike Yarwood, the impressionist. In an effort to keep the wolves from the door she returned to the old job, mainly in working men's clubs and Jackie started introducing her.

'Mum said she couldn't get him off the stage in the end,' says Laurie. 'But he never really looked back, and he was a very funny man. He didn't do men only, he was very moralistic and shy. I never heard him say the f-word.'

Andrew Blanchflower was unaware of his father's place in the history of Manchester United until the family moved into the Royal Oak at Millbrook, near Stalybridge, in 1968 – the year of United's first European Cup Final win – and the customers began to remind him.

'To us he was just Dad. He never came across as a celebrity and I don't think they were in those days. The celebrity he enjoyed was in the last ten years of his life and I think people made a fuss of him. People used to come into the pub to see him. But "Jackie Blanchflower, Busby Babe", didn't mean anything to us. I remember going to the twentieth centenary [sic] match in 1978 when I was about fifteen and they were shouting his name, and he came on to the pitch and they were shouting "*One Jackie Blanchflower*" and I was like this, going down the wall, I was so embarrassed. That's how I was with it. He stayed passionate about football, like anyone who has ever played. He would have played for nothing, which is what they did in them days.

'At work they would ask: "Are you any relation to Danny?" and he would always say "no relation", and that was what Munich took away from him; the chance to be as big as his big brother. That team would have achieved it, he was part of something that was going to be really big. That was what he was bitter about. He never thought he got dealt a great hand. Munich was the start of a bad run for him. People used to say "you were lucky". Some luck.'

The Blanchflower children came to dread every 6 February. Laurie says: 'It was never a normal day and never a normal night and even the couple of days leading up to it were bad. Every time he shut his eyes he must have seen it. He wanted to be left alone with his memories, he wanted to be with the lads who died, he would rather have gone with them than ever play again.'

'Every 6 February was a nightmare to us,' adds Andrew. 'He used to say he wished he was dead with all his mates. It was a real bad time especially when we lived in the pub because he would have a drink and that worsens the problem. We used to keep away from him. Munich was the biggest part of their history and my dad was part of it although it cost him. In the end it cost him his life because someone told him it would take ten years off his life. The damage he did to his renal organs, the liver, kidneys and that.'

Unlike some of the other survivors, notably Viollet and Foulkes, Blanchflower resisted the temptation to sell his medals and mementoes, although some of them are now in the club museum.

Laurie says: 'Dad put bits and pieces into their museum but we don't get a penny in royalties. They could write to us and let us have a ticket at least.' Andrew adds: 'There was a load of other stuff, caps, medals and that and I was thinking of putting them all in the museum.' To which Laurie promises: 'Over my dead body!'

Three days after the crash and just before Jimmy Murphy had escorted Gregg and Foulkes from the Stathus Hotel to Munich railway station en route to Manchester via Rotterdam, the chief surgeon at the Rechts der Isar Hospital, Dr Georg Maurer, took all three on a tour of the wards containing United's stricken players.

Gregg says: 'Jimmy wanted me and Bill to go to the hospital so the ones that were alive could see us and not realize what was going on. It makes good sense now. In the hospital

Dr Maurer went to each bed. Kenny Morgans didn't have a mark on him and was totally unconscious. Johnny Berry had wires everywhere. Maurer went through them: Matt and Duncan, 50-50, Jackie Blanchflower and Scanny, thumbs up, Dennis Viollet, OK. Then he got to Johnny Berry and he sighed and said: "I am not God."'

Berry, outwardly, the smallest and frailest of the players, overcame the most fearful odds to survive, but like Blanchflower paid a fearful price for his 'luck'.

Born in Aldershot on 1 June 1926, the winger had been rejected by his home-town team as 'too small to make a footballer', and when he left school it was to become a trainee cinema projectionist. But he went on to make 276 appearances for Birmingham City, his only other senior club, between 1951 and 1958. Like many of his United team-mates, Berry played for the British Army team during the Second World War and his talents as a winger – pace, a shrewd football brain and the ability to get to the byline and deliver damaging crosses, caught the eye of Fred Harris, the Birmingham captain, who was in the same Army side in India.

It was these talents, plus some memorable performances against his side in the First Division, that persuaded Busby, looking for a replacement for the ageing Jimmy Delaney, to splash out £27,000 to take him to Old Trafford in 1951. Berry, like Byrne, thus bridged the gap between the title-winning side of 1952 and the Babes of 1956.

A chirpy, effervescent and ever-optimistic character, Berry's name is seldom remembered by the Old Trafford cognoscenti, but he was, in fact, one of their most successful buys ever, collecting three championship medals, four England caps and a Cup Final runners-up medal in 1957. His worth to the side is best summed up by John Doherty: 'Someone like Beckham couldn't hold a candle to Johnny Berry. Beckham bends the ball and I say two things: I bet £100 he can't kick it straight because the ball is too light and b) I'll give him an old-fashioned case ball and see how many times he scores with it. The ball swerves, he doesn't make it swerve. I look at Beckham and he can't go past anyone. I have never seen him beat anyone, he doesn't have the pace to do it; Giggs has all the pace in the world and his final ball is outrageous. Beckham is supposed to be the best crosser of the ball, and he's OK when he's got the time and space. But could he do it with the full-back tackling him? Johnny Berry could. Johnny could get to the byline and bend his toe round the ball. And he scored goals [forty-five in 276 appearances for United, including the winner in the quarter-final of the European Cup in 1957 against Athletic Bilbao]. When he was at Birmingham he used to make United's life a misery.'

The player's injuries at Munich included a fractured skull, a broken jaw, mouth injuries leading to the removal of all his teeth, a shattered elbow joint and a broken pelvis. Like Blanchflower and Busby, he was given the last rites by a German priest. He was in a coma for two months and when he did return to Manchester three months after the crash he knew nothing of it, or of the death of his team-mates. The Berry family's agonies, however, were just beginning. It was plain he would never play again, but a light had also gone out elsewhere.

Scanlon recalls a former players' dinner where 'Johnny was spilling his soup all down his chin' and Gregg recalls the tiny winger's – he stood only 5 ft 5 in and weighed under ten stones – forlorn attempt to re-integrate himself at Old Trafford: 'His foot–eye coordination had gone, but still Johnny came down to Old Trafford, the little sick man, like a wee cock sparrow, to try and train with Jackie. It was pitiful. Johnny was so small and they couldn't tell him, or wouldn't tell him, that he had damaged this thing to his brain when he got the knock on his head.'

There was little in the way of compassion from Berry's employers. Within twelve months the Berry family, Johnny and Hilda along with their eight-year-old son Neil, had been ordered to leave their club house just off Davyhulme Road (to make way for Shay Brennan) and his employment cards arrived in a brown envelope through the post. He worked for a time as a labourer at Massey Harris in Trafford Park before returning to his home town of Aldershot, where he went into business with his younger brother Peter, another former professional footballer, selling sports clothing.

Neil, his son, who went on to a successful career as a head teacher in Buckinghamshire and later Central London, was to give a hint of the family's sufferings when he said: 'My father went away to play football as one man and returned as a completely different person. He was never able to drive or concentrate for any length of time, and though as he grew older his injuries caused him increasing pain, he seldom complained. The Munich air crash changed the life of my family forever. We were all personally traumatized by it and suffered indescribable private grief.'

Given the reality of United's inability, or unwillingness, to help it was inevitable that Hilda Berry would become extremely embittered. She never forgot or forgave the club and the strength of her feelings is best illustrated by the fact that when her husband died in 1994, Harry Gregg had to telephone her and ask if it would be all right for the old players' association to send a bouquet of carnations – red and white carnations – to the funeral.

10

FORTY YEARS ON

Manchester United was not the first major football team to be wiped out in an air crash. Nine years before Munich, on 4 May 1949, the plane carrying the Italian champions Torino FC back from a testimonial match in Lisbon ran into dense fog and plunged into the basilica on the Superga hill above the club's home city. There were no survivors among the thirty-one passengers on board.

The parallels between Superga and Munich are remarkable. Torino's home stadium, the Filadelfia, was bombed and badly damaged by the Royal Air Force during the war and the club had been through a major rebuilding process with the help of a wealthy benefactor, the industrialist and former Torino player Ferrucio Novo. The Italian players who died were all household names and, it is said, bonded by a friendship that many commentators saw as the over-whelming factor in their five consecutive Serie A titles and an unbeaten record at the Filadelfia that stretched back for six years. Of the eighteen players on the plane, eight were current internationals, including Valentino Mazzola, their celebrated captain. Mazzola, like Roger Byrne, was a figure of considerable charisma and authority on and off the field. He was married with a young son, and in the same manner as Bobby Charlton, that son, Sandro, proved an enduring, and popular, link between the club's past and present as the Torino director of football. The Torino side of the Forties also possessed a fair share of rascals, one of whom, Mario Rigamonti, invariably arrived for training on a motorcycle. Quite often, like his Salford alter ego, Eddie Colman, he was late. Striker Guglielmo Gabetto, nicknamed 'The Baron', part-owned a bar in the city and was once arrested after loading the team coach's boot with contraband cigarettes following a fixture in Trieste. This, and other evidence of eccentricity and individuality, along with their unmatchable abilities on the field, earned Rigamonti, Gabetto and their team-mates a place in the hearts of Italian football supporters which lasts to this day.

Like Munich, Superga is haunted by darker ironies. Torino had flown to Lisbon as last-minute substitutes for Bologna and, as post-war pioneers in the use of air travel for distant away fixtures, had endured two horribly memorable flights that came very close to disaster on an earlier tour of South America. Most of the players dreaded flying. No one has ever been able to explain why the aircraft crashed above Turin when its scheduled landing point was Milan, eighty miles to the north-west.

A small party of journalists had travelled with the team to and from Portugal on the doomed aircraft and the coach was an Englishman, Leslie Lievesley, who had once been on the books of Manchester United and who was born in Staveley in Cumberland, six miles from where Roger Byrne's widow, Joy, lives today. One injured Torino player, Sauro Toma, should have made the flight but was left behind for treatment. Toma went home from the Filadelfia to find forty people waiting in the snow and rain outside his house in the Turin suburbs and when he rushed over to the Superga it was to meet fans streaming down the hill, most of them in tears. The sixty-three-year-old former national coach, Vittorio Pozzo, who had built his successful Azzurri side around the Torino team, undertook the task of identifying the bodies.

Like Manchester, Turin saw an outpouring of grief in the days after the accident that hadn't been witnessed before, or since. The coffins were displayed in the Madama Palace before individual burial and the city came to a stop as half a million people flooded the centre to mourn their heroes. Pozzo, who by then was a sportswriter on *La Stampa*, was to write later: 'There were kilometres and kilometres of women and babies crying. There was all Turin: I thought there was half Italy. It was my Torino, the team I gave so much help to build. I called ten out of eleven of them in our national selection, all at the same time. I remembered, while walking, the dead and the pranks: Mazzola and his family matters, Rigamonti and his motorbike, Grezar and his sad smile, Gabetto, The Baron, always facetious. After the ceremony, I felt like I was in the world of dreams, so many thoughts I had in my mind. An old military fellow, an alpine captain who, in uniform, followed me all the way, brought me home. Not a word, in the car. The silence was enough. On the house door he embraced me. I threw myself on the bed and wept.'

The dead players have never been forgotten. Fausto Gobbi, a lifelong Torino fan who has lived and worked in Manchester for over twenty years and goes to Old Trafford to see his 'second' team whenever he can get a ticket, says: 'The Grande Torino's memory is part of Italian football, not only of Toro fans, and the anniversary of the crash is marked on 4 May every year when the current team, without exception, climb the hill of Superga to attend a religious ceremony at the end of which the current club captain reads the names of the immortal champions, one by one. The church is always full and the emotion deep. Unfortunately, after that, Torino has won only one more league title and now is faring very bad. They never have lived up to the reputation of their famous forebears.'

In terms of their fortunes on the field, the same conclusion could not be drawn about Manchester United, and many attached to Old Trafford, in particular the various boards of

directors since 1958, will see the disparity in the two clubs'
playing successes as the reason Torino are not enshrined in
football and sporting memory in the same manner as their
English counterparts. Others will insist just as vehemently
that it was the tragedy, and the subsequent rise from the
ashes of Munich, that has made the Manchester side a
household name worldwide and earned them support, admi-
ration and riches on an unprecedented scale.

Sandy Busby, who grew up with many of his father's
eponymous Babes and could be forgiven some sentimental-
ity about Munich, says instead: 'It's a load of bollocks to
suggest that United are so well known and popular because
of the crash. The reason we are the most famous club in the
world is because we have won so many things. Don't forget
that, in 1949, 81,000 people were at Maine Road watching United against Yeovil Town. When they played away
there were lock-outs every time, so something was there.'

Harry Gregg disagrees: 'My wife Carolyn is not into
Manchester United, she is totally resistant to Manchester
United, and she said to me many years ago: "You know,
Harry, if Manchester City had crashed at Munich they
would have had the love United have." I was so upset at
the time, scandalized, but in a way she was right. That's
how she sees it, that's the way maybe the rest of the world
should see it.'

David Meek, who covered United for over thirty years
as a sports reporter on the *Manchester Evening News*,

believes that 'Munich is one of the factors for them becoming a club of worldwide renown. The emotion and drama of Munich opened United to a lot of other people worldwide, they became fans. There was the human aspect of it. The good die young.'

Gobbi, however, offers a few other suggestions: the lack of mass communication in the Forties which kept news of the Torino tragedy and its aftermath localized, and the fact that the Italian players who died were so much older than the Babes – the eldest, Ruggero Grava, was thirty-three and Mazzola himself thirty – making the sense of loss less acute. Of the eighteen dead players, too, only two could claim a measure of indigenousness in that they graduated through the Torino youth team; the remainder were bought from other Serie A clubs. But Gobbi's most damaging assertion is that 'Torino kept their memories of the accident low-key. The team are commemorated once a year, but that is it. The families have always been left alone with their grief.'

'Yes, they do wheel us out from time to time,' says Irene Beevers with a tiny smile of resignation. The 'wheeling out' for the sisters and mother of David Pegg and the other families down the years have generally been for the anniversaries of Munich – the tenth, the twenty-fifth, the thirtieth – when not all of them have felt inclined to attend, preferring a less public form of grieving. But there have been regular invitations to various club rites, including the unveiling of the Matt Busby statue outside the Megastore in 1997, the opening of the first museum in 1986 and the ceremony, performed by Pele, which saw the inauguration of the new version in 1998. There have also been a succession of other ancillary events to which the families have been asked along to add suitable gravitas to proceedings, notably the ceremonial opening of a housing estate in Newton Heath, United's original home. Instead of the usual Lake District beauty spots or well-known trees, the local council had decided to name the thoroughfares after the team: Eddie Colman Close, Duncan Edwards Court, David Pegg Walk and so on. Over the years the Peggs, Taylors, Whelans and others have dutifully turned up without complaint. They have not always, however, been consulted on some of the other aspects of United's market-ing offensive.

After the first United museum was opened, in 1986, Irene Beevers, who was on holiday in Wales at the time, happened to pick up a newspaper out of which fell a glossy insert advertising United's latest attraction. The picture used to entice customers to the museum was a large head-shot of her brother, David.

'I couldn't believe it,' she says now. 'Wouldn't it have been polite to have asked us? If my mother had seen that she would have had a fit. She would have fallen apart. I did write to Ken Merritt [the club secretary] and asked him would it not have been polite to ask permission? I got a letter back from his office saying words to the effect that the company owns the copyright to the pictures and doesn't have to ask anyone. They also said the museum is just to honour the players, not sell tickets or make a profit. To be honest, I haven't got the emotional energy to go on with that, so I just left it.'

Her husband Jack, a bluff former miner, is less inclined to let things lie: 'It really annoyed me that someone, somewhere at Old Trafford had all this worked out. It was obvious that some legal expert had been through all the implications with a fine toothcomb. Someone in that organization has it all sown up. It's calculating without any feeling.'

In July 1991, the club sent what amounted to a circular – formatted and with a space left at the top for the name of the recipient – to Jessie Pegg and the other Munich families suggesting that as there were plans to extend the museum they may care to contribute memorabilia and artefacts from their dead sons and brothers. The letter, on the official, embossed United notepaper with the distinctive red crest, was signed by Bobby Charlton, who by then was a director of the football board and over the years has been the main conduit between club and Munich relatives. Most of the families, rightly concerned about the possibility of burglary and the high cost of insuring priceless memorabilia, complied and forwarded jerseys, medals and other items which are on display today. Officially, these are 'on loan'; there has never been an offer of payment and the only cost to the club is the insurance.

'There are items in the museum,' says Joy Worth, the widow of Roger Byrne. 'Most of Roger's things, all his caps, his medals. It got to the point where we couldn't afford to insure them. But I don't think they belong to us, they belong to the supporters.'

The museum, whose entrance is next to the Red Café in the North Stand, is spread over three floors and has a separate room dedicated to Munich. Some may see exhibits that include the passport of Eddie Colman, the player's provisional driving licence and a letter from the secretary Les Olive to a fan informing him that 'a specialist had informed Johnny Berry that he will unfortunately never play again'– in dubious taste, ghoulish even, but there is little doubt that whoever designed the interior has a fine sense of theatre.

Albert Scanlon's passport is open to show a stamp issued by the customs at Belgrade airport, close by Duncan Edwards's poignant telegram to his landlady informing her that the plane had been delayed. A recording of the original BBC radio broadcast giving news of the crash is played constantly in the background for the benefit of visitors and there are also cuttings from newspapers of the time. MATT '50-50'; EDWARDS 'GRAVE'; BERRY 'COMA', says one duplicate front page from the *Manchester Evening News*. Perhaps Fausto Gobbi is right to point out that tragedy is saleable. As United's official website says: 'Stand still as the world did, and listen to the tragic news report that shocked everyone who heard it. Through newspapers and photographs we are reminded of the people who died on that fateful day of 6 February 1958. Understand the club's determination to carry on, knowing that those who were lost would have wished it.'

This sort of fevered marketing has proved a resounding success with around 200,000 visitors a year attracted to the museum which currently contributes £1.3m per annum to the club's corporate health, a small chunk of Rio Ferdinand's salary if you like. But as Laurie Blanchflower points out – and here is one of those other niggling anomalies that attends Manchester United's dealings with the survivors and families of the Munich dead – 'Most of my dad's stuff is in there, but If I want to go and see it I have to pay a fiver.'

Munich, and virtually everything connected with it, has become a business in its own right. After the then chairman of Real Madrid, Santiago Bernabeu, died in 1998 his family decided to auction a bequeathed tapestry of silk and gold braid which depicted most of the lost United players (the face of Edwards is missing as he died after the work was commissioned). For years it hung in the stadium chapel, but it went on sale in 2001 with a reserve auction price of £20,000. The auctioneers were Mullock-Madeley, of Wolverhampton, and United apparently had first option

The aftermath: The rescue teams comb the wreckage on the runway at Munich.

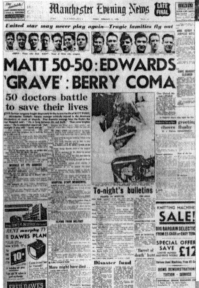

The bulletin: the *Manchester Evening News* kept its readers in touch on a daily basis.

The stricken: Matt Busby fights for his life in an oxygen tent. He was given the last rites twice.

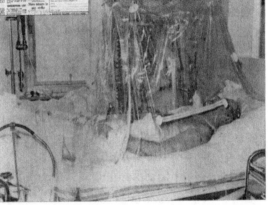

On the road to recovery: Albert Scanlon and Dennis Viollet lived to play another day, but the psychological scars were to last forever.

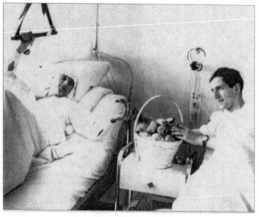

Survivor: A reluctant Bill Foulkes, soon to be made team captain, was persuaded to return to the crash scene the following day.

Grounded: Assistant manager Jimmy Murphy arrived in Munich to take Gregg and Foulkes home. This time they travelled by train.

München

Hoek van Holland

ABOVE LEFT: The return: Busby arrived back at Old Trafford in May, 1958, ready to build a new team around Bobby Charlton.

ABOVE: First gong: Two months later, a filled-out and healthier Busby received the OBE, watched by his proud son Sandy and wife Jean.

ABOVE: They also serve: Amy, the skipping waitress at Ringway Airport, was a favourite of the Busby Babes, Duncan Edwards in particular.

RIGHT: Born again: Joy Byrne gave birth to Roger Jnr 38 weeks after the United captain died at Munich.

LEFT: Safe hands: Ray Wood was a reliable goalkeeper in the Babes era, but lost his place to Harry Gregg post-Munich.

BELOW: Well saved: The logo on the Villa Park stand has it right as Gregg flies to the rescue against Fulham in the FA Cup semi-final, March 1958. A patched-up United side went on to reach Wembley where they lost to Bolton Wanderers.

LEFT: Only a rose: A solitary flower marks the fatal spot at the old Munich airport on the anniversary of the crash, February 1998.

BELOW: Return to Munich: At the invitation of UEFA, the survivors went back to the city for the European Cup final in May, 1997. Left to right:: Kenny Morgans, Bobby Charlton, Harry Gregg, Jackie Blanchflower, Dennis Viollet, Bill Foulkes, Ray Wood and Albert Scanlon. Johnny Berry had died three years earlier; Blanchflower and Viollet were soon to follow.

LEFT: Flowers of Manchester: Bobby Charlton, United's enduring figure, lays a wreath at Old Trafford on the 40th anniversary of Munich, a duty he has performed countless times.

RIGHT: Lest we forget: Duncan's mother Sarah Edwards pays her own tribute underneath the Munich plaque outside Old Trafford.

BELOW: Germany remembers: Joy Marsh (Byrne), Bavarian politician Hermann Memmel, Sir Alex Ferguson, United secretary Ken Merritt, Bayern Munich legend Karl Heinz Rummenigge, Old Trafford chief executive David Gill, Munich's deputy mayor Gertraud Burkert and Sir Bobby Charlton at the ceremony to unveil the new memorial at Trudering in September, 2004.

ABOVE: Forever young: In his 21 years on earth Duncan Edwards earned immortality, with his statue in Dudley a permanent reminder of the town's favourite son.

RIGHT: Without farewell: Duncan's grave in Dudley remains a place of pilgrimage for football fans from all over the world.

FEB 6th 1958

MUNICH

Roll of honour: The Munich
clock at Old Trafford, right,
and the plaque which
commemorates the eight dead
players and three officials at
the ground.

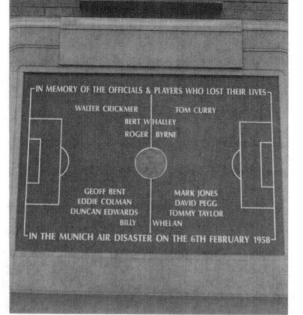

IN MEMORY OF THE OFFICIALS & PLAYERS WHO LOST THEIR LIVES

WALTER CRICKMER   TOM CURRY
BERT WHALLEY
ROGER   BYRNE

GEOFF BENT   MARK JONES
EDDIE COLMAN   DAVID PEGG
DUNCAN EDWARDS   TOMMY TAYLOR
BILLY   WHELAN

IN THE MUNICH AIR DISASTER ON THE 6TH FEBRUARY 1958

to buy. Mullock-Madeley director John Mullock, however, caught the populist mood of the times with his claim that Victoria Beckham was also in line to 'buy it for Becks'.

Busby's old Jensen Interceptor – a strange choice of transport for a man noted for his frugality and lack of ostentation – has done the rounds for years, advertised as 'Sir Matt Busby's former car' and the manager's old houses on Wilbraham Road and King's Road in Manchester have several times been marketed as 'the house that Sir Matt lived in'.

'The first one on Coleridge Road, too,' points out Sandy Busby. 'Years later the estate agent flogging it got in touch with us, through the club, asking if the Busby family would like to buy it back. But they were asking way over the odds for it.'

In 1995, Bonhams of Knightsbridge were instructed to auction the manager's original 1946 United contract and the eight-page document was knocked down to a mystery buyer for £4,000. The identity of the seller, and how it came to be in their hands, remains a mystery.

All of this could be put down to modern-day fiscal opportunism, or a combination of need and greed, but when the crutches Busby used to get around after he left the Rechts der Isar Hospital were offered for auction forty years later it was clear that matters had strayed too far into the realms of dubious taste, a point of view only endorsed by the auctioneer, Colin Palmer of Philips, who claimed:

'The significance they hold is very high as they symbolize Busby's recovery, both emotionally and physically.' The crutches were expected to raise £1,500, but ultimately failed to attract a buyer. Unabashed, the seller returned them to the market in April 2003.

One of Tommy Taylor's first England shirts, bearing the number nine, also went under the hammer in 2001, the sellers being the Nottingham experts in sporting memorabilia, T Vennett-Smith. Taylor's father had sent the shirt to a family friend at the time of the player's funeral and over four decades later it was available to the highest bidder. The reserve price was boosted, however, by an addition to the lot – a private letter from Charlie Taylor which read: 'I am sending you a souvenir in remembrance of Tommy – it is one of his international shirts. I hope you will live a long time to remember.'

A photo album that had once belonged to Eddie Colman also went on sale in January 2002, at the order of the Australian owner. The item had been bequeathed to the owner by his uncle, who in turn had been given it by the former United chairman Louis Edwards. How Edwards acquired it also remains a mystery.

There have been books on the Busby Babes and Munich too numerous to mention and every one ever written on Manchester United has carried at least one chapter on the disaster with the same graphic details regurgitated. Few of them have received approval from the survivors. Albert

Scanlon, in particular, is dismissive of journalist Frank Taylor's account in *The Day a Team Died*, wondering how a man who had been so seriously ill for so long after the crash remained lucid enough to recall, and record, verbatim conversations in the hospital. Gregg also disputes certain of Taylor's recollections of the accident, notably the journalist's written appreciation of the efficiency displayed by the German airport authorities.

'He claimed there was a fleet of ambulances on the runway but if that was the case how come we ended up on the way to hospital in the back of a coal truck?' demands Gregg. Taylor, who died in 2002, was the only journalist to survive the crash although he suffered appalling injuries to his right leg and left arm and surgeons for a time considered amputating either or both of the limbs. His book is a moving testament to the power of the human spirit, but cuts no ice with the likes of John Doherty, who says: 'Frank made a fortune out of Munich.' Taylor was awarded an OBE in 1978.

Books apart, there have been full-scale stage plays about the Busby Babes, one-man shows about the Busby Babes and TV documentaries with, once again, the families and survivors asked to trawl through tragic recollections on camera. Irene Beevers was interviewed by a film crew making a TV biography of Sir Matt Busby in 1999, with the producer insistent that this was a tribute to the late manager. As it turned out, the documentary, part of the BBC2 *Reputations* series, was an attempt to destroy

Busby's standing and prove that the kindly, avuncular figure of legend was, in fact, a ruthless opportunist.

Viewers were invited to be astonished that a football manager was prepared to transfer-list and sell players who were not performing to his expectations, and the film-makers eventually arrived at the verdict that in his fifty years in football at the highest level Busby had actually managed to make a few enemies. But there was plainly another, more dubious, agenda.

Irene Beevers says: 'On that programme they wanted me to talk about Matt Busby trying to persuade the pilot to take off because of the Wolves match on the Saturday. I told them: "I am not an expert on aeroplanes. My father liked Matt Busby and I am not going to sit here and slag him off. As far as I am concerned you are here under false pretences."' Whereupon, she and her husband Jack showed the disappointed documentary-maker the door.

Roger Byrne Jnr was aware at the age of six that he was the son of a famous father when the first journalists arrived, on 6 February, to ask him to go down to the field at his primary school in Urmston, and kick a ball around for the photographers.

'It has dropped off a bit now but it used to be virtually every February that we would be contacted by somebody,' says Roger without the least sign of disapproval. 'They would ask: "Can I come and have chat a or discussion with you?" I have been out to Munich with the *Daily Mail* and I found that very traumatic. The reporter and photographer were the same people who had been chasing the Yorkshire Ripper.'

The fabled story of Manchester United being what it is, various Hollywood-style blockbusters have been mooted from time to time. In one aborted film, the casting of the leading roles was sensationally inapt: the playwright Harold Pinter in the role of Sir Matt, Caroline Quentin from the TV sitcom *Men Behaving Badly* as Lady Jean and Alfred Molina, perhaps better known as a Middle Eastern villain in *Raiders of the Lost Ark*, as Walter Crickmer. Christopher Eccleston, who featured in *Shallow Grave*, *Let Him Have It* and television's *Doctor Who* was tipped to play Duncan Edwards.

A rival version was to feature Liam Neeson as Busby, but the 6 ft 5 in Irish star of *Schindler's List* and *Rob Roy* eventually turned it down. In 2000, pre-production of another film was announced, this one building the Munich story around a fictionalized player, 'Stewart Scott'.

Paul Nicholls, of *EastEnders* fame, was cast in the starring role as a teenage striker, 'a protégé of Duncan Edwards', whose career is ended when his leg is injured in the crash. Bill Foulkes was one of the first to raise his voice in condemnation when he said: 'The team was a whole. We didn't have any fictional characters. We want real people – they were real people. I just don't agree with it all. I feel they shouldn't try to exploit something as tragic as that. It was a disaster for English football and for Manchester United and for families and everybody.'

The prospect of seeing their loved ones immortalized on celluloid by soap stars left most of the Munich families less than overjoyed. 'How would they portray our Liam?' asks Rita Whelan. 'We dreaded the thought because they would probably have had this Irish character going round saying: "Jaysus, begorrah, sure I must be off to mass now, boys."'

Then there are the heroes by proxy. These are the journalists who insist they would have been on the flight to Belgrade but for last-minute change in sports editors' scheduling and at least two players who have made similar claims.

In his autobiography, *Harry's Game**, Gregg rails against a former team-mate, 'an after-dinner speaker who has lived on it for years, claiming he would have gone to Yugoslavia but for injury'. Gregg would not name the player in print, but Wilf McGuinness, one of the original Babes and later the United manager, is still a man much in demand at corporate hospitality functions where he regales the audience with tales of his days at Old Trafford. McGuinness has also been quoted, more than once, as claiming that he was listed to go to Belgrade, and by implication, possible death. In fact, he was not even a first-team regular at the time and the man who should have gone as cover for Jackie Blanchflower and Mark Jones was Ronnie Cope. In the end, a minor injury to Roger Byrne forced Busby to name an unwilling Geoff Bent in the party. Cope,

---

* *Harry's Game* (Mainstream Publishing, 2002)

to his eternal credit, has resisted the temptation since then to tell the world about his own narrow escape.

Gregg has also long disputed Foulkes's version of events on the airfield. After Munich the man who took over from Byrne as captain became, like Gregg, a symbol of the United regeneration, of the club's unwillingness to founder after one of the most savage sporting tragedies ever, a hero. Foulkes has been reported several times in print as saying that he saw Gregg carrying a baby out of the wreckage, but this claim is rubbished by the Irishman who insists that his team-mate had obeyed Captain Thain's order to get as far away from the wreckage as quickly as possible. Occasionally his verdict has been more brutal: 'You should have seen the big fucker run,' says Gregg.

Matters between the two men finally came to a head at United's training ground, The Cliff, in 1975, when Gregg was on the club's coaching staff. A stormy confrontation ended with Gregg telling Foulkes 'that he had been living a lie for seventeen years'.

'These people are only too happy to live on the memory of Munich when it pays them,' Gregg adds. 'To some individuals it has become an industry. Before I die some of them will be saying they were the pilot of the aircraft.'

While a small corporation of people have sought to profit, either materially or otherwise, from Munich, the relatives of the dead players never have, although many suffered – and continue to suffer in some cases – indescribable mental and material distress. Some parents, notably the fathers of Eddie Colman and Roger Byrne, and David Pegg's mother, never really recovered; June Jones had been left with a two-year-old son, Marion Bent a five-month-old daughter. Joy Byrne discovered shortly after Munich that she was pregnant.

All the bereaved, without exception, have never seen a debt incumbent on the football club. As Christy, John and Rita Whelan point out, all the money in the world is not going to bring back their dead brother and Joy Worth says now: 'We have never asked anything of Manchester United and never would.' Her son, too, is happy to help propagate the memory of the father he never saw without condition, insisting: 'I don't get fed up with the anniversaries and things like that. I am wary of the negative angle to Munich, but as far as I am concerned everything has always been done very tastefully. The museum particularly. It would be easy to brush it all under the carpet.'

Irene Beevers believes that 'initially they could have done a bit more, been a bit more supportive but it was a major event that people were not trained to deal with. If someone had come along and put their arms round you and said "we will look after you" it might have been different.'

If death at Munich has left an immutable scar on the lives of the bereaved families, survival has proved almost as difficult for many of the players who climbed, or were hauled, out of the wreckage. Berry and Blanchflower never played again and many commentators believed that the accident took something irretrievable out of the play of Scanlon, Morgans and Viollet. Certainly, in playing terms they did not survive too long after Munich as Busby gradually moved them on without ceremony.

This, and the fact that as time went by United's executives and major shareholders enriched themselves on the club's deeds while many of the survivors struggled by on minimal resources, seemingly forgotten, was to cause increasing rancour. The thought that an institution valued at one billion pounds could offer only the occasional match ticket – the universal currency of football clubs – was to make even men as amenable as Albert Scanlon, Jackie Blanchflower, Kenny Morgans and Johnny Berry deeply embittered.

Most accepted, as Irene Beevers and others had, that United's administration had been wiped out in the crash, and that there were few precedents to help an institution cope with such a tragedy, but resentment grew to an intolerable extent as the years went by.

The measure of this animosity has long been recognized by people close to Manchester United, if not by the average fan on the terraces. One veteran Stretford Ender I spoke to was convinced that both families and survivors had been granted some sort of lavish club pension for the forty-five years since Munich, while Irene Beevers has become weary of the number of people who approach her in Highfields cemetery to remark: 'Haven't United done a good job looking after your David's grave?' Herbert Barker, the second husband of June Jones, has consistently been accused of 'landing on his feet by marrying me', according to June.

Employees, and those close to Manchester United, have become adept at treading the fine line between loyalty to the club and outright sympathy for the plights of families and survivors. David Meek chronicled the playing deeds of the club for almost four decades and his name is still better known in Manchester than several of the past, and even current, players.

Born in York, Meek arrived in the city in 1956 to work as a leader writer and political columnist on the *Evening News* and when Tom Jackson died at Munich, he was asked if he would cross the editorial floor to the sports desk as emergency cover.

'Then they started on the FA Cup run; I decided to stay on and covered them for thirty-seven years until I retired. Match days, particularly Saturdays, were amazing when I look back now. There were two football papers in the city (the now defunct *Evening Chronicle* was the other) and at the match you would have an open phone line from wherever United were playing to a copytaker at the other end taking down your running match report. The intro was done ten minutes before the end, and the paper was out on the streets fifteen minutes later.'

In his lifetime as a follower of Manchester United it was natural that Meek would become a friend and confidant of most of the great players who passed through the Old Trafford gates as well as various members of the board and managers. Dennis Viollet called him 'Scoop', but for a specialist sports reporter in the regions a happy and unbroken working relationship between local club and local newspaper is a prerequisite and far more important than news-gathering skills.

In fact, the one time Meek overstepped the mark in the eyes of the club by breaking an exclusive they wanted to suppress, Busby banned him from the team bus, for life.

Meek, in many ways, should have written this book, but a man who still works for the *United Review*, contributes to the club website and is the author of works such as *The Official Manchester United Greatest Players*, may have found it difficult, if not impossible.

Seated in the living room of his house in the south Manchester suburb of Sale, Meek still chooses his words carefully when discussing Manchester United and the aftermath of Munich, particularly the long-standing ill feeling of the survivors:

'A few of them felt more could have been done for them but they tended to judge that by the light of today,' he says. 'In those days, and we are talking a long time ago, half a century ago, when people were involved in an accident or tragedy the lucky ones were the ones who survived, the unlucky ones the ones that died. But in those days people didn't rush around in quite the same way and help. Nowadays if there was an equivalent tragedy there would be funds, counsellors' assistance all sorts of help. We have become more caring. It's not that people turned their backs on the Munich crash.

'There was a Lord Mayor's Fund, which admittedly didn't amount to very much, and insurance was not very sophisticated in those days. They didn't get much when you consider what happened. As they grew older they would maybe judge it by more recent events and a lot of them got quite bitter.'

Gordon Taylor, the current secretary of the Professional Footballers' Association, puts it another way: 'I can imagine that some of the former players look at the multi-millionaires at Old Trafford today and think that "they owe quite a bit to us". It happens to a lot of sportsmen. They think it will go on for ever and then suddenly it ends and it is like a cold bath, it's like your wife has left you and there is no money. Suddenly it can be a battle.'

After Munich, there were a lot of battles ahead as the golden, guileless days of the Busby Babes suddenly gave way to squabbles over restitution by various factions. A measure of compensation was available to relatives and survivors immediately after the accident, but that was desperately modest even by the standards of that day. Despite Busby's claims to his board that he had managed to build a team worth over £200,000 the Munich side were hopelessly under-insured for just over half that amount and the payment was shared equally between club on the one hand and families of the lost players on the other.

The day after the accident the Lord Mayor of Manchester, Leslie Lever, launched an appeal which was to raise over £52,000 from benefactors as diverse as Great Universal Stores, the *Manchester Evening News*, Harry Vos, gown maker of Spear Street, Manchester, and the inmates of Strangeways Prison. The total was divided between families and survivors in a ratio dependent on their circumstances. Albert Scanlon, for example, received less than £300. There was little help from within the game. Today, the Professional Footballers' Association, the sport's trade union, can offer a lump sum of four times total earnings for death in service and a comprehensive insurance scheme; in 1958 this sort of aid was unattainable. After the accident, the then secretary of the PFA, Cliff Lloyd, advised families and survivors to see a solicitor and sue the airline for lost baggage and BEA eventually paid out amounts that varied between £60 and £100.

United's main claim against BEA was to drag on interminably for over ten years, the delay being in the main due to a dispute over the precise cause of the accident. The Munich airport authorities insisted that it was due to Captain Thain's error in not de-icing the wings (in which case BEA would be deemed liable). The airline and Thain, who fought long and hard to clear his name, were equally adamant that it was slush on the runway (the airport being responsible for such contamination). BEA eventually settled out of court in 1968, for around £35,000.

The crash was also to have international repercussions and sour relations between the British and German governments. Official declassified papers, released in 2001, revealed that while separate British and German inquiries disagreed about why the crash happened, Thain had succeeded in forcing the then British prime minister, Harold Wilson, to set up a fourth, German, inquiry, in 1968. With the 'slush on the runway' theory the inevitable verdict – a German official had inspected the plane immediately after the crash and seen no ice on the wing, evidence which the Bonn government had suppressed – the Foreign Office then stepped in to say that the report 'cast doubt on the propriety of the original investigation' and there would be 'a risk of serious damage to our relations with Bonn'.

Another FO official insisted that 'our assessment is that the Germans are likely to react very sharply indeed to the publication of evidence or findings which would impugn the integrity of their investigation'. In April 1969, the attorney general, Sir Elwyn Jones, decreed that 'a report which made an attack on the German inquiry would be an unhappy outcome'.

As it was, the Germans never re-opened their inquiry and Thain, who had been dismissed by BEA in 1960, could not sustain his campaign. He died of a heart attack in 1975, at the age of fifty-three, one of the last victims of Munich.

Throughout the years that followed the air crash the club's attitude to families and the survivors has remained oddly ambivalent. On the one hand, Joy Byrne and Roger Jnr were allowed to stay indefinitely in their club house in Flixton for what she describes as a 'peppercorn rent' while the maimed Jackie Blanchflower, whose first daughter Christa was born just after Munich, was asked to vacate his. As was Berry, a decision which sparked a resentment in his wife Hilda which lingers to this day and prompted the family to cut off all relations with the club. Scanlon, too, struggled through a succession of low-paid jobs when his career ended, but still the club resisted mounting pressure to help the needy financially. Ultimately, it was to take forty years for them to agree to a benefit and even then it was not at the instigation of Manchester United.

In 1997, the eight living survivors, Bobby Charlton, Viollet, Scanlon, Foulkes, Ray Wood, Blanchflower, Morgans and Gregg – Berry had died in 1994 – were invited by UEFA to the European Cup Final between Juventus and Borussia Dortmund, in Munich's Olympic Stadium.

Gregg takes up the story: 'I had been a guest at the Player of the Year awards dinner in London and when I came back my wife said Ray Wood had phoned. I rang him back and he said: "Have you had this beautiful letter?" And it was a magnificent letter from UEFA, basically saying that "we believe you are people who made the European Cup what it is and we would be very honoured if you would be our guests, the eight survivors, at the final of 1997". They added that they had been in touch with Manchester United and they have agreed.

'But then Woody said over the phone: "We have to shaft these so-and-sos", meaning United and trying to get some sort of compensation. But I said: "I am no Solomon. They are too big, you can't do anything against them and if you think I am going to stir up shit for a few quid you have the wrong man. If you want to discuss it we will talk about it when we get to Munich."'

And so the grizzled survivors went back to the city where their lives had been irrevocably changed so long before. It was at once an emotional, traumatic and occasionally controversial return. Blanchflower was plainly quite ill and Viollet's erratic behaviour offered a serious portent to the brain tumour that was soon to kill him. It was also the last time that many of them would see Wood.

They obligingly posed for photographs and gave a press conference where Foulkes once again gave his version of events on the airfield, only to be contradicted by Gregg at the other end of the table.

The seven former players – Charlton was not present – got down to the nitty-gritty in the day before the final, gathering in the Ibis Munchen Messe hotel to decide how to squeeze some indemnification from their former employers.

Gregg adds: 'We called the meeting, and my opinion was that the club's too big, so we had to get the PFA in. Kenny Morgans was plainly very bitter about it all and next to speak was Popular Bill [Foulkes] who said: "I agree with Greggy." Next was Woody, who pointed out how they had shat on us down the years and the last to speak was Blanchy, who insisted we couldn't do it on our own. "I don't even go back there any more," Jackie said. Some didn't want Bobby there. But whether you like him or not, he was there at Munich and should have been part of it. So I phoned Charlton and gave him the right to be there or not and he decided not to. The next step was to contact the PFA.'

From then on, things began slowly to escalate. The head of the Manchester United Former Players' Association, David Sadler, became involved and a committee comprising David Meek, former Busby Babe John Doherty – who had been asked by Gregg to represent him and the other survivors – and the PFA's Gordon Taylor, was constituted.

Meek says: 'People like Jackie [Blanchflower] had always struggled physically, and it had left him embittered as well. Embittered with life in general and, yes, the club would be included in that. I took the view that it was better late than never and forty years was going to be a milestone that was going to be observed so why not do something for those still around? In 1998 they were all coming up for retirement age and not a lot of them had been in the kind of jobs that would give them a decent pension and that kind of thing. I am thinking of Albert Scanlon who had been a security guard, then working in a bakery, and things like that. It was timely in that sense and a bit negative to say it's too late, it's gone on too long. Some people focused on the belief that not a lot had been done over the years. In fact, the club have quietly helped quite a lot of them, but it's not the sort of thing they have made publicity about. It is not true to say they had been neglected.'

United plc, however, were offered by the author the opportunity via the chief executive Kenyon to list examples of their largesse towards the Munich victims, but Kenyon never responded to e-mails or phone calls. Harry Gregg has remained just as questioning.

'John Doherty reported straight back to me,' he says. 'I said I want projection etc. I want to see gate receipts, sale of programmes, they had to forward all receipts of money going out. I said I realized that for forty years Manchester United FC never wanted to accept the Munich tragedy as part of their lives; maybe the plc would like to make up for the shortcomings of their predecessors. Some people there did help in their own small way. But it took two years to pay it out.'

Taylor, a former Birmingham, Bury, Bolton and Blackpool winger ('all the B's' as he likes to put it) runs the PFA from a luxurious office suite just off Oxford Road in the centre of Manchester and can rightly claim to be one of the most powerful and astute men in the game. But even Taylor can hardly have imagined the personal and political complexities of the task that lay ahead.

What he did realize from the start was that diplomacy was more likely to win the day than outright confrontation and, slowly but surely, he brought pressure to bear on the club.

He says: 'John Doherty and David Sadler told me they were not getting very far raising funds for those who had survived and families of the dead and they came to see me. I took them to the boardroom over the road and we contacted the club. Ken Merritt was very helpful, so was Ken Ramsden. Martin Edwards was still chief executive.

'Apparently they had been pressurized by different relatives and different players. Harry Gregg, as is part of his nature, was very bitter about the way they had been treated because the club had gone on to expand. He always thought a lot of it was due to him.'

Taylor's strategy closely involved Bobby Charlton and early in June 1997, after a charity golf match at Didsbury attended by both men and some of the survivors, Taylor wrote to the most high-profile of them to try and move things on. Still, the club prevaricated with Merritt advising Taylor on 26 June that 'no firm decision has yet been made by the board about the testimonial' and that it was 'a complex issue'.

How complex it all was soon became clear. Eventually, early in 1998, Doherty went to see the chief executive at his £1m home in Wilmslow, the Beverly Hills of the Cheshire plains.

'I wanted to ask Martin Edwards about the likelihood of some sort of benefit game for them,' says Doherty. 'He said: "But why now, John? Why now, after all this time?" And I said: "Because they are fucking skint, that's why."'

11

ERIC THE READIES

The man with the power to change that state of affairs was already a millionaire several times over when Doherty arrived at his doorstep on his Munich begging mission. Martin Edwards's wealth owes much to his three decades of involvement with Manchester United and if there is one man who has come to represent the unacceptable face of football capitalism it is Edwards. He may not deserve the epithet of 'that bastard' given to him by one supporters' website, but Edwards would certainly be in the running, if we are to believe the numerous United fans, for the award for the most reviled administrator in the club's history, probably just edging out his father, Louis.

The average terrace dweller has always had problems with boards of directors and football chairmen, usually questioning why anyone should be granted the power to run their club when they could do it so much better, but

Edwards consistently attracted more bile than most. This undoubtedly has less to do with the way he ran the club (although he did make some disastrous managerial appointments, lost the club a small fortune in a farcical flirt with basketball and fell out with Sir Alex Ferguson over the purchase of new players), and more with the fact that most of his power was, in the eyes of the support, inherited.

Much of this, too, owes much to inverse snobbery – fans are always ready to point out that Edwards went to a rugby-playing public school where he attained just six O-levels, a lack of achievement heightened by his rather vague air – rather than ire about the way he ran the club. United, after all, did enjoy a success unprecedented in English football during the Edwards era.

But mud sticks. Louis Edwards, who was head of a flourishing meat packaging business, was appointed a director of the club after an emergency board meeting the day after Munich, filling the opening left by the death of George Whittaker who had suffered a heart attack in his London hotel room just before the match at Highbury five days earlier.

A firm friend of Busby's, his previous attempt to join the board had been vetoed, so it would be reasonable to say that Louis Edwards had been favoured by circumstance. He made the most of his opportunity, building up his shareholding over the next decade by the simple expedient of purchasing them from fans and widows of fans until, at a cost estimated at around £750,000, he held an overwhelming majority of over 70 per cent . . . and total power at Old Trafford.

By 1962 he had become the third largest shareholder in the club, and his brother-in-law, Denzil Haroun, also had a large holding.

By 1965 he was chairman and United launched along the mercantile path that saw the country's first hospitality boxes, the souvenir shop and various 'executive' watering holes. The white picket fencing that Duncan Edwards had once vaulted so nimbly for the benefit of the TV cameras, was pulled down to make way for advertising hoardings. This was to be Martin Edwards's inheritance.

He was born in 1945 at Adlington, near Macclesfield, and attended Terra Nova at Holmes Chapel, one of the most expensive preparatory schools in the country, before going to Cokethorpe public school on the edge of the Cotswolds in Oxfordshire. This privileged, middle-class upbringing, as might be guessed, was to sit uneasily with the average Manchester United fan. When it was later discovered that he had played rugby at Cokethorpe and had dropped out with six 'O' levels to join the family company run by his father and uncle, the sneers intensified.

His rise was inexorable. In 1970 the Manchester United board, chaired by his father, voted him in as a director at the age of twenty-four and ten years later, following the death of Louis, Martin Edwards was the chairman and majority shareholder. Middle class, well dressed and hand-some – although an uneasy performer in front of the media – Edwards was to guide the club through thirty years of varying success until he was unseated.

The most serious accusation ever made of both Martin Edwards and his father, however, has been their unwilling-ness to bend a knee to history, and Munich in particular. Or at least only when it suited them. While Merritt and his assistant Ken Ramsden have pushed through a few hand-outs to survivors and families – notably to Dennis Viollet's second wife Helen when he was traumatized by a brain tumour in 1998 and faced massive medical bills in the United States – Edwards, asked in 1997 if United had helped any of the families or survivors, replied vaguely: 'Oh yes, one or two.'

In many ways Edwards, who became chief executive in 1982, filled the gap between the old-style local merchant/ chairman and the modern-day career bureaucrat like his suc-cessor as CEO at Old Trafford, Peter Kenyon, who joined the club from Umbro, the sportswear manufacturers. Many have questioned the Edwards motives down the years.

In 1991, he oversaw the club's flotation on the Stock Market, which saw the club valued initially at £18 million before in 1997 they were able to announce record profits of £27.6 million, making them officially the biggest and richest club in the world and Edwards one of the richest chief executives in European sport.

Edwards had consistently proclaimed Manchester United the love of his life, but has also demonstrated by his actions over the years a morbid fear that the value of his monopoly of shares would collapse overnight. On three occasions he has attempted to sell the club: once to the fraudster Robert Maxwell, in 1984, and then five years later to Michael Knighton, a Yorkshire schoolmaster turned property developer. After Knighton's takeover was announced – for a startlingly paltry £10 million– Knighton dribbled and headed the ball the length of the pitch for the benefit of the Stretford End. His juggling with figures, however, proved to be far less assured and his bid collapsed shortly after his two major backers dropped out. Knighton had to be content with a somewhat less glamorous United, the one at Brunton Park, Carlisle, where he managed to take them to the edge of non-league football in his eight years there as chairman, chief executive and, at one time, head coach.

Unabashed by the bile that descended on his head after this fiasco, Edwards supported BSkyB's attempted takeover in September 1998. This valued the club at £623.4 million, but the bid fell foul of a combination of fan backlash and the Monopolies and Mergers Commission and foundered.

Edwards was to have his day in the sun. A month after Rupert Murdoch's attempt to buy the club was aborted, United beat Bayern Munich in the Champions' League Final in Barcelona to complete an historic treble of European and FA Cups and the League Championship.

On the return from Spain Edwards rode triumphantly through Manchester atop the team bus, the value of his holding soared again and a year later the club officially broke the £1 billion value barrier. Still, Edwards continued to unload the shares in the 'love of his life', banking £41 million by selling to friends of the horse-racing grandees John Magnier and J P McManus and another £21 million to the Scottish property magnate, Harold Dobson.

He stayed fiscally cute to the end. When he finally stepped down as chief executive in 2000, he retained the position as chairman of the football club and continued to be paid a large salary for what amounted to two days work a week plus a package that included a car to the minimum value of a Mercedes S500, 25 days' holiday a year, sickness benefits, company pension, personal health and life insurance, and medical expenses for him, his wife and two children.

His fall, and final severance from the club, came in November 2002, when police questioned him over Peeping Tom allegations involving a woman guest at the Mottram Hall Hotel, Prestbury. The woman claimed she was followed into the hotel toilets and then realized a man she didn't recognize was peering at her from under the door of the cubicle. Police inquiries later identified Edwards, a regular visitor to the hotel, as a suspect and a spokesman for Cheshire Constabulary confirmed: 'A fifty-seven-year-old man from Wilmslow has been cautioned in respect of Section 5 of the Public Order Act.'

Manchester United claimed that the incident would not affect Edwards's position at the club, but within a short time Kenyon, who earned a mere £325,000 a year at Old Trafford for this sort of thing, summoned Edwards to his office and told him he had to step down.

This, then, was the man who in 1998 was asked to approve a benefit for the families and dependants of Munich, ease the last years of a number of former employees and, perhaps, win himself some much-needed fan approval. Both he and the club botched the opportunity in spectacular style.

After Edwards and the United board had agreed to hold a benefit for the Munich Disaster Fund, the club and the fund committee began to cast around for a suitable date, and suitable opposition. Real Madrid, Red Star Belgrade and Bayern Munich were mentioned as potential competition, all three clubs possessing the appropriate historical links with United. But, in fact, none of them were approached and it came as a surprise to many when early in February 1998, the *United Review* announced: 'We are delighted that Eric Cantona is coming back to Old Trafford to say the kind of goodbye to Man United supporters that we all wanted from him at the end of last season.'

The Munich testimonial, in fact, was to become a supporting act to the official farewell to the Frenchman who had left the club so peremptorily a year previously to pursue a career as a film actor, although the *United Review* did add as an afterthought: 'Some say forty years is a long time to wait for a testimonial match but it is, in our view, a very appropriate moment as many of the people involved approach the age when they must think about their pensions!'

Harry Gregg was scandalized. 'The opposition were going to be Red Star, Real Madrid or Bayern Munich. No one else was mentioned and Joe Public bought tickets on the strength of that. Then I read in the paper that Eric Cantona was coming. Diabolical.'

According to Edwards, it was Cantona who made the initial approach with a request for the chance of a suitable valediction to his adoring fans.

'Eric approached me about wanting to come back to play a farewell match at Old Trafford,' said Edwards. 'Trying to fit in the Munich match was difficult, so to organize two was impossible. When we got Eric's letter it seemed obvious to combine the two.'

According to some Old Trafford sources, Edwards had always felt a lingering guilt about the manner of the departure of the former captain. Cantona had undoubtedly been one of the most influential figures in the playing history of the club after his arrival from Leeds United in November 1992, helping them to four Premiership titles and two FA Cups. But his insane drop-kick of a pop-eyed, loud-mouthed fan at Selhurst Park during the match against

Crystal Palace in January 1995 was rewarded by an eight-month ban from the game and although he was to win two more championships, Cantona's career went into decline. The thrust-out chest gave way to an expanding waistline and a double chin, and following a row with the club over rights to have his name on replica shirts in the newly opened Megastore, Cantona, in May 1997, suddenly announced his retirement.

Now he was coming back.

The obvious concern of the Munich dependants, and the survivors headed by Harry Gregg, was that the testimonial would become simply a tribute to Eric Cantona, but Doherty offers his justification: 'There was talk about Real Madrid and Bayern Munich coming and there was a problem there because they were in the Champions' League and so were United,' says Doherty. 'I told some people to be realistic because they wouldn't come over free of charge, either. We had to get bums on seats. We talked about who could come and who couldn't and then the Cantona thing came into the equation. I think Gordon Taylor spoke to Cantona's agent or brother and it went from there. We had a special programme done which was a replica of the programme we had used in 1957 for the players' pool and I think it was the biggest-selling programme ever at United.'

Taylor worked long and hard on other aspects of Munich fund-raising. A charity night at a local hotel raised £500, donations of £1,000 each came from Nestlé UK and the Telegraph Group and a contract was signed with Video Collection International to make a film of the event. He hardly missed a trick. When he heard that the *Manchester Evening News* were planning a special supplement to mark the occasion he wrote to the editor suggesting that they may like to make a donation to the fund. The newspaper duly forwarded a cheque for another £1,000.

An actual date for the fixture, however, was proving more elusive. With the fortieth anniversary of the crash approaching, a memorial service in Manchester Cathedral was already planned for 6 February, with a home league fixture against Bolton Wanderers the following day. After that, the nearest free date in the calendar was 24 February. But, on 15 February, Barnsley held United to a 1–1 draw at Old Trafford in the fifth round of the FA Cup and a replay (won 3–2 by Barnsley) was scheduled for 25 February. Then, with £15,000 of tickets already sold, Cantona announced that he would be out of the equation until late summer as he had signed for a starring role in the movie *Mookie*, playing a boxer on the run from gangsters. His co-star was a talking chimpanzee and Cantona gave the news in typically enigmatic fashion – giving his 'press conference' to a group of high-school students in the Dordogne. They asked if the main character was really a self-portrait of a proud, morally correct, generous personality who was essentially modest and easy-going. 'Let's say that all these characteristics are a fair reflection of what my friends and family think of me,' Cantona replied. Eventually, the testimonial was postponed until 18 August.

The delay at least gave Taylor and his committee time to deal with some contentious issues, not least of which was a final decision on how the money should be divided. There were complications. Both Ray Wood and Dennis Viollet had divorced their first wives, both of whom could justifiably have claimed to have borne some of the anguish after the crash, helping nurse husbands back to health and to cope with the mental trauma.

Elizabeth Wood, who had campaigned long and hard in print for some form of restitution from the club, eventually consulted a solicitor who bombarded Taylor with letters demanding that she be recognized.

Once news of the testimonial became public there were other representations, with letters to Edwards from relatives of dead passengers and crew, including one from the family of the steward, Tommy Cable, and some of the journalists. Edwards simply passed these on to Taylor and the PFA to sort out.

Taylor confirms: 'There were a number of applications from other people, including relatives of the dead journalists. I had to tell them that because we were the PFA the fund could only apply to players and their dependants. The terms of the benefit and who would be entitled to shares had been decided and published in advance. It's sad, but that's the way it is.'

Eventually, the testimonial committee decided that there would be one share for each club passenger still living, one for the widows still living of club passengers who died and that in the case of a club passenger who had died, and had no widow still living, his share would go to any living child or children in equal measure. If there were no children the share would go to any living parent or parents in equal shares and if there were no children or parents then his share would go to any living brothers or sisters in equal shares.

The final part of the agreement, and one that would prove the most contentious, decided that 'if none of the above applies to a share then the share will be paid by the committee to one or more charities of their choice'.

The match, when it eventually went ahead on 18 August, almost seven months after the anniversary of Munich, featured a Manchester United XI against a European XI. As many had feared, it turned into the Eric Cantona show, the tone being set at once when Mick Hucknall, United's most public supporter and the lead singer of Simply Red, crooned *Every Time You Say Goodbye* to the Frenchman. Hucknall, had replaced at the last minute the Urmston-born tenor Russell Watson, who had originally been asked to sing during the half-time interval. Watson, a life-long Manchester United fan, was devastated.

Cantona appeared hand in hand with his ten-year-old son, Raphael, the boy symbolically clad in a replica red number ten jersey. There was a minute's silence which most supporters assumed was for the Munich dead but in fact was for the victims of the Omagh bombing three days earlier, and United also chose the occasion to make a few presentations – to the Reserve Player of the Year (Michael Twiss), Young Player of the Year (Wes Brown) and for the Sir Matt Busby Player of the Year (Ryan Giggs) before the opposing teams appeared.

United duly won 8–4 and Cantona did a lap of honour before, in the words of one fan, 'he took the microphone and spoke to us of Munich and of his wish to do something to help commemorate it and raise money for the families and survivors. He then explained that he had left because he had lost the passion for football – he had had ten years in football, and the five years he had spent at Old Trafford were the best of all. He told us he loved us and that who knows, he may see us again soon.'

Three weeks after the testimonial match, and with Cantona back in France working on his film, Taylor, in his role of chairman of the Munich testimonial committee, received an invoice from Pascal Carbon of CMC International, 7 Rue Montpellier, Neuilly/Seine, Paris, for £90,555.01 which revealed for the first time exactly how much Cantona's appearance had cost the testimonial.

Carbon, a former French international, was Cantona's agent for footballing matters at the time, and had merely done what every good agent does and attempted to maximize the earnings potential of his client. This included a lengthy correspondence with Taylor about who would be entitled to the TV and video rights, but in the end an agreement was reached to pay the Frenchman's expenses.

These expenses included the hire of a Lear jet to ferry friends and family from Paris to Manchester and a hotel bill at the De Vere Mottram Hall Hotel in Cheshire, a five-star establishment set in 270 acres of rolling Cheshire countryside with its own seventy-two-hole golf course, which amounted to £15,869.94.

Cantona himself stayed for three nights while others in his extended party remained for four or five nights. Some of the survivors wondered why, if United were so keen to say farewell to Eric in such style, did the club not foot his bill? Why did the testimonial fund have to pay for the fifty-one Capo de Monte figurines, at over £100 each, for each of the competing players? And why did the club bill the testimonial for over £15,000 for refunds of tickets from the postponed match five months earlier when it was they who had postponed it? A significant gesture, surely, would have been just to write that sum off.

Some questioned why Charlton should be entitled to a share, others why Busby's children, Sheena and Sandy, should be granted over £20,000 each. Eddie Colman, as it turned out, too, had been virtually the last of his line with no close dependants and, as per the terms laid out originally, Taylor had given his share to charity, the Royal Manchester Children's Research Fund and the NACRO Community Link Project both benefiting. Some of the survivors, who were not consulted, were unhappy about this, believing that Colman's share should have gone 'back in the kitty'.

Taylor says: 'Look, a United team played Eric's team, we had a packed crowd and made a presentation afterwards and raised virtually £1 million that was split equally without any discrimination or discretionary judgement equally between those who survived and immediate relatives of those who died. The problem with Eddie Colman was that he had no strong family links so made a donation to Salford where they have a scheme for football initiatives and kids who can get back into sport and in danger of going off the rails.

'As for Cantona, people can be happy about it or not, but it would be nice of them to be gracious that he was responsible for a lot of people turning up. Rightly, he wanted provision; he brought a lot of his family and brought a team over and they didn't hitch-hike. They came by plane. We gave a great deal of time and trouble and didn't get thanks from everybody.

'Some, but not everybody. Bobby Charlton was always very quiet about it and some felt he shouldn't have a share because he has done so well since. Again, that might be a bit of jealousy or bitterness. He took his share and rightly because it becomes a bit of a means test otherwise. Considering what he did for the team it's fair enough, he is a great ambassador for English football, and I won't have a word said against him.'

Doherty, too, was left embittered by the whole experience. He says: 'Someone asked me what was your aim and I said it was to raise £1 million and we did that. I thought we did a very good job. As for thanks, I think the club got three or four letters, I didn't receive one. I'm not sure about Gordon.

'The thing that has always hurt me is that not one of those players I played with took the trouble to either pick up the phone to me or just drop me a card to say thank you. Where they were kidding themselves was that clubs like Real Madrid would travel with all their management and players, clubs who were millions of quid in debt, and play a game and pay their own expenses. With Cantona the end justified their means.

'Would they have rather Cantona not played and we had 30,000 people there? By the end I was sick of it. There were even some people who thought that the ones that died shouldn't get anything, just the ones living. And why not Matt's family? They were just as entitled as anyone else. Matt had been injured in the crash after all. When you get down to it you have to be harsh and say that players like Jackie and Johnny had their careers ended by injury, just like me. But if someone came to me tomorrow and asked if I would do it again, I probably would.

'Harry [Gregg], of course, finished up rowing with me, because he thought it was a disgrace what we had paid Cantona. I told him: "Harry, you are not living in the real world, it doesn't happen like that." But we were not speaking for a while until he rang me out of the blue and demanded to see the accounts. I told him "I have worked fucking hard for this, and not even charged the price of one phone call. Everyone will get a set of accounts."'

When the accounts did appear after the fund closed late in 2002 they showed that with Cantona's cut taken out, along with £8,461.11 for the Inland Revenue, £5,560 for the Capo de Monte figurines, the £15,018 refund to United and ancillary expenses for printing of the programmes, posters and stationery, £47,283.89 remained for each dependant or divisions of a dependant. Or almost exactly half of what Cantona received.

The first cheques went out in October 1998. Albert Scanlon bought himself a new telly and sent a donation to the Omagh bombing appeal of 1998 and to a collection raised for a steward who had died at a Coventry City match the same year.

'The money paid for my mum's nursing home fees,' says Irene Beevers. As for the Whelans, Rita Whelan spoke for many of the families when she said: 'We were not bothered about the money. All the money in the world could not bring our Liam back.'

Nor did it quench the bitterness felt by survivors like

Gregg and the Munich testimonial, which should have been an occasion of grateful remembrance and a celebration of the lives lost was ultimately submerged in bile. 'It has all been so much PR bullshit' was Gregg's caustic verdict and he may have had a point.

By August 1998, United's combined wages bill amounted to over £30 million a year, Martin Edwards had personally made £38 million in sales of shares in the club and six months later, in February 1999, a survey conducted by Deloitte and Touche on behalf of the football magazine *Four Four Two* worked out that United's turnover in that year amounted to £87.9 million. It was, officially, the biggest, and richest, football club in the world.

Alongside this, the £47,000 received by a number of people whose lives had been traumatized by Munich does seem small beer. And the long-awaited windfall came far too late for some.

12

THE TROUBLE WITH HARRY

Harry Gregg concluded his autobiography with the poignant words: 'On the beach, in the still hours before the world awakes, I often see their faces. They are all young men. We all are.'

But, of course, he is not. His seventieth birthday, in October 2002, fell midway between two operations for removal of a bowel tumour and slowly he has had to rationalize, albeit with some reluctance, that while the Babes may be immortal the ones left behind are not. His runs along the local strand have slowed to walks.

If he needs any further conviction he only has to look down the list of players who boarded the ill-fated BEA Elizabethan at Ringway Airport all those years ago and realize that, with Sir Bobby Charlton, Albert Scanlon, 'Young Kenny' Morgans and Bill Foulkes he is now one of only five remaining survivors.

Gregg's candour has made him many friends, and some enemies, down the years. He is still revered in Northern Ireland and is highly respected in Manchester, and in Germany.

Virtually unscathed in the crash, Gregg famously ignored Captain Thain's warnings and went back into the blazing wreckage to help team-mates and to rescue a young woman and her baby. But the description of 'hero' sits uncomfortably with him, as he has long been at pains to point out.

'Is Harry still wearing that bloody tracksuit?' Albert Scanlon had asked. Indeed he is, a smart, dark-green one with the insignia of the Irish Football Association on the lapel. Gregg was still recovering from his operation when I went to see him at his home in Antrim but remains a tall, upright and athletic figure and still with the tight-lipped, frowning glare of a thousand photographs.

Like Scanlon, Viollet and his rival for the United jersey in the Babes era, Ray Wood, he is also a heavy smoker. The tight, curly hair is speckled with white now, but Harry Gregg still looks like a man you would rather have as a friend than as an enemy.

'If Harry likes you you will never know, but if he dislikes you will soon find out,' said one close friend.

He lives in a large, converted farmhouse on the Antrim coast with his second wife, Carolyn, who is from the north of England and is one of the Maunders, the noted Lancastrian home-builders. His five daughters and son are away now but there are horses in a field behind the main building and some land. Gregg is plainly comfortably off in comparison to some of his former team-mates.

After he left United for Stoke City in 1962 and later hung up his playing boots, he managed to stay in gainful employment, notably as a much-travelled coach and more recently as a hotel owner in Portstewart, just up the coast from his present home. When we met his autobiography had just been published, preceded by a newspaper serialization focusing on his allegations that some United players took bribes in the 1960s. He didn't name names, but it was inevitable that other newspapers would ask him to and a telephone rang constantly in another room throughout the four hours I spent with him. He ignored it.

Harry Gregg was born at Tobermore in County Derry on 25 October 1932 and arrived in Manchester in December 1957, via Coleraine, Linfield and Doncaster Rovers. A joiner by trade, when he signed for Doncaster he joined his great countryman, and boyhood hero, Peter Doherty, who at the time was manager at Belle Vue. To this day, Gregg's opinions of Doherty are laced with appreciation, gratitude and love. Doncaster were not the minnows in those days they have since become and in fact the club had their own floodlights long before Manchester United installed theirs. He made his first-team debut early in 1953 against Blackburn Rovers, that debut being marked by a typical Gregg scenario, a determined charge out of goal that wiped out opposing centre-forward Tommy Briggs and a Doncaster defender. To many, Harry Gregg became the living, breathing justification for the old adage about all goalkeepers being crazy.

It is an oddity about Manchester United that while a veritable conveyor belt of talent has rolled off their youth production line from the 1950s to the present day, the club has never managed to produce an indigenous world-class goalkeeper. Gregg, who was signed for what was then a world record for a goalkeeper of £23,500, had followed Ray Wood, who signed from Darlington and before Wood, Reg Allen from Queens Park Rangers was in goal.

At Doncaster, Gregg's athleticism and command of his area were unquestionable, but Busby had, as always, done his homework about the player's character, seeking verbal references from boyhood friend Jackie Blanchflower. When he arrived in Manchester Blanchflower and his wife Jean were waiting at Victoria Station, along with Busby, Jimmy Murphy and a platoon of the Manchester press.

'That was a nice gesture but typical of Matt because he knew I had played with Jackie as a schoolboy,' says Gregg. 'I had just had five years at Doncaster and got an accrued share of a benefit which came to £33. Now I was going into the big time. I got on great with the lads and I think they liked me. The most difficult ones to get to know were Bill Foulkes and Bobby Charlton, but I had played against Duncan, Tommy, Roger and with Jackie so it wasn't as if I had never met them before.

'You see running on to that pitch for Manchester United? You could not describe it. The most important man in football, though, is Joe Public for if they don't like you, that's it. But the United fans took to me, mainly because I carried on like a bloody idiot; I spent more time out of goal than in. The first game I nearly took Duncan's head off, but that was my way.'

Gregg arrived at Old Trafford in December 1957, a few months after Wood had sustained a broken cheekbone in the 1957 FA Cup Final. The two Manchester clubs fared badly with their goalkeepers at Wembley. City's Bert Trautmann famously suffered a broken neck in the final of 1956, Wood was knocked cold twelve months later and Gregg himself was bundled over the line along with the ball, by Bolton's Nat Lofthouse three months after Munich. Both of the charges would not have been allowed today, although many would say that in Gregg's case it was a form of poetic justice, a view tacitly admitted by the Irishman when he appeared on a *This Is Your Life* which honoured Lofthouse in April 1993. 'I spent most of the rest of the match looking for a chance to even the score,' he says.

* * *

Munich apart, most of Gregg's memories of United in the Fifties are happy and fulfilling ones. 'The lads were typical of the time. David Pegg was a real Jack the lad, a flashy dresser and an outgoing young fellow. Liam and Roger were two of the nicest men God ever put on the earth. Eddie Colman fancied himself as Frank Sinatra with his pork-pie hat.

'They were not angels you know. I remember in the dressing room when we played Luton Town and we got a draw when we should have won. Someone piped up: "Who was picking up the full-back?" and war broke out. It wasn't all sweetness and light. What typifies United to me is that at Doncaster Monday, Tuesday, Wednesday and Thursday we would train. I got to Manchester United and we had Monday off and on the Tuesday morning a big coach would take us to The Meadows and we trained there. It was a doddle. Duncan, of course, wanted to go back in the afternoon.

'At Doncaster, drink was a taboo; when I got to Old Trafford there was a crate of beer against the kicking board in the dressing room.

'Tommy Taylor was a very quiet big man, him and Jackie were very close. Bobby came into the team the day I went there, when Matt dropped Ray Wood, Jackie B, Johnny Berry, Liam Whelan and David Pegg and brought in a fellow called Gregg, Mark Jones, Kenny Morgans, Bobby Charlton, and Albert Scanlon. That team continued all the way to the accident, except they brought Johnny Berry back to give Kenny Morgans a rest. I still talk of him as young Kenny to this day.

'We spent all the time at Davyhulme golf course on the day before a game. We were all members. We would eat steak and egg or chicken. Drink sherry. Play cards. I was playing snooker there when I realized I had a hole in my shoe, this big star with the world record fee. Then you would drive down Warwick Road in the bus with a big crowd, and stars in your eyes. Frankie goes to Hollywood, Harry goes to Hollywood.

'I moved from Doncaster the Sunday before the crash and moved into Jack Rowley's old house, then Jeff Whitefoot's. Jackie and Jean were living on The Quadrant, just by the cricket ground, and one day a neighbour rang the police to say there was a strange man trying to break in. It was their lodger, me.

'I also stayed with Roger and Joy Byrne in Flixton. Their dog pissed on the carpet in my bedroom and I was terrified they would think it was me.

'I remember the caper on the last night in Belgrade. There was a model Sputnik on rails going round the room, I can see it to this day, and I recall Mark Jones singing *On Ilkley Moor Baht 'At*. I remember who went back to the hotel and who didn't. I remember Jackie Blanchflower hanging off a balcony pissed out of his mind. We played cards through the night till five in the morning. Dennis

Viollet and me were rooming together; some of the others had gone out to the embassy.

'Then I remember in the hotel after the crash watching a flake at a time come down and the families arriving and having a bad time with the media. Jimmy Payne, the best friend of Duncan, I threw him out of the lift. We became good friends later, but it was a bad scene at the time. I remember a photographer in a long coat taking pictures. The saddest thing, apart from the carnage, was that I got sick and tired of going up and down in the hospital lift. I decided to walk up the stairs which were not well lit and before I got to the top flight I could hear this terrible sobbing from round the corner and I looked round and Jimmy Murphy was sat halfway up the top flight crying his eyes out. I just turned and went back down.

'I have won every honour Ireland could give me. I was born in Ireland, Irish blood runs through my veins and as far as I am concerned one of my jerseys is worth ten of Ray Houghton's, and I feel the same about Manchester. Once I wrote down on a piece of paper, the first team, second team, A and B team and I put an asterisk against Gregg, an asterisk against Wood, asterisk against Taylor and asterisk against Berry. The only ones they had bought in. All the rest were Babes.

'United, I have got to be proud I was there. There was the freshness of youth and it was all down to what Matt Busby created with a bunch of lads. He broke the mould and even before Duncan Edwards came in he went against everything football stood for at the time.'

Determined to abide by his oft-stated principles concerning Manchester United and Munich, Gregg had no intention of attending the Munich testimonial, but in the end, as he puts it: 'I had no choice.' A phone call from Manchester to his home from Jean Blanchflower two days before changed his mind: Jackie was dying. Gregg had been photographed – Blanchflower with his shy, dreamy smile and Gregg with the baleful stare he was to effect in virtually every subsequent picture, for even at the age of fourteen this was plainly someone you did not mess with – in the same Northern Ireland boys' team fifty years earlier and the two Ulstermen had been friends ever since. Now Jackie wanted to call on that friendship for the last time and asked Gregg to meet him at Old Trafford to say farewell.

Andrew Blanchflower says: 'Dad was dying in 1998, although I don't think he was as aware of that as we were. The papers said it was cancer that killed him, but it was acute liver failure in the end. I never saw him drink excessively, but he damaged a big part of it at Munich, and he only had one kidney. The legacy of Munich got them all in the end. At first I didn't want him to go because we are making an exhibition of a dying man and that's not fair.

But once we had got there it was all right. Mick Hucknall of Simply Red told me: "Your dad was my hero."'

Jackie Blanchflower died on 1 September 1998 but the family's run of ill fortune continued. His widow, Jean, developed a circulatory problem over the next three years and this led to both legs being amputated and, ultimately, a fatal heart attack.

Laurie Blanchflower, however, is convinced that 'when Dad went half my mum died, too. They were inseparable. I think she just gave up in the end. It was such a shame because things could have been so different. Dad was at that stage where he was turning into a really nice old man, really caring, making a fuss of the kids, his grandchildren. It robbed them of that. I think he liked being recognized, just going to the working men's club on Saturday. He had time for everybody. I never heard anyone say they didn't like my dad.

'At least he did make it back for the 1998 testimonial and it was good for him to see his old team-mates. But it was also very sad because it was too late for him. If they had done something like that years before I'm not saying he wouldn't have died; I am just saying he would have had a better life. Families have had to suffer, too. We have had to suffer. United didn't do enough for them, but could you ever do enough for them? How do you put a price on something like that? It makes you wonder though: were the ones that died the ones that got away with it?' Laurie christened her son Jack Blanchflower Barton: 'Someone thought we were sad. They thought it was because we supported United, but I thought it was one way of remembering Dad.'

Ray Wood, Gregg's predecessor in the United goal, had already survived one heart attack before his death in the summer of 2002 and had remained a smoker most of his life. His first marriage to Elizabeth ended in acrimonious divorce and in the years since Munich he enjoyed an amazing nomadic career which took in coaching appointments in America, Cyprus, Greece, Canada, Kuwait, Kenya, the UAE and Zambia.

After Munich he never managed to oust Gregg and Busby moved him on to Huddersfield. From there he joined Bradford and Barnsley before qualifying as an FA coach and setting off on his travels.

He came back to Britain in 1982 to settle in Bexhill-on-Sea in Sussex and took up golf with a vengeance. He ran a sportswear business in Bexhill, then took charge of a suit department for a store in Hastings for nine years before retiring in the mid-Nineties. When he had his face crushed at Wembley in 1957, the United coaching staff persuaded him to go back on to make up the numbers as no replacements were allowed in those days. Eventually, after a warm-up in a Wembley car park where a young boy with a football had asked if he 'fancied a kick about' he returned to the pitch . . . first on the wing, then for a short period back in goal. Later, he was to relish the answer to a frequently posed quiz question: which keeper started and finished an FA Cup Final between the posts and didn't let in a goal, yet went home with a loser's medal?

Whether it was a result of the assault at Wembley, or other factors, his form slumped subsequently and on 21 December 1957, Busby dropped Wood, who had joined the club from Darlington as a teenager, in favour of the hungry Irishman. The two rivals remained friends until Wood's death. Most obituaries, wrongly, labelled him a Busby Babe.

He remained his own man to the end, like Gregg unwilling to suffer perceived injustices. One of these was an attempt by his ex-wife to sell his football medals, which were due to be auctioned by Sotheby's in 1999. Wood knew nothing of the sale until alerted by a local newspaper. Sotheby's told his lawyer only that the medals, including a gold league championship medal won in 1957 and valued at £4,000, had been offered for sale by a private collector.

'I was appalled when I heard about this,' said Wood at the time. 'I want those medals to go to my two daughters. The last person I am aware of having my medals is my ex-wife. She kept them when we divorced. But they are still my property and I didn't give them to her.'

Wood employed a lawyer to recover his trophies, which also included a Football League representative medal, from his former wife, but he never received them. He was most distressed about a gold medal he won as a sprinter in his native North-East. He had used the prize money to buy his daughter's first pram.

Elizabeth Wood said: 'If Ray wants to stop the sale, he has the right. I used to collect his medals and shirts and I stored them when we split up. But now I have closed the book on Ray. It is a long time ago and I have no idea about his medals.'

In the end, Sotheby's aborted the sale.

At his funeral in East Sussex, in the summer of 2002, they played the Morecambe and Wise theme song *Bring Me Sunshine* and a week later Debbie, one of his two daughters, sent Albert Scanlon a card which concluded with the words: 'Thanks for all the good times you had with Dad.'

Viollet, the great striking buccaneer of the Busby Babes, had gone three years earlier. Munich had left him seemingly unscathed although many were to remark that his personality changed drastically.

'I think he realized that life was worth more than football,' says his great friend John Doherty. 'He got in with a different crowd after Munich and it came down to a simple thing with Dennis: either he was boss or Matt was boss. In the end there was only going to be one winner. Matt got rid of him because of his nightclubbing, he thought him a bad example to kids. I think after the experience of Munich Dennis was determined to lead life to the full and that was a life that didn't necessarily square up with being a top-class athlete. He was moved on before he was finished as a footballer which he showed at Stoke.'

Viollet had long been a regular on the Manchester United nightclub scene and was spotted regularly in Deno's, Mr Smiths or the Continental throughout his career. This had never sat easily with Busby, who was kept well informed by a succession of the fan-spies who have plagued United's playboys down the years.

Eventually, in the summer of 1961, Busby informed Viollet that he was selling him to Stoke where he enjoyed a glorious Indian summer to his career under the steward-ship of an equally gregarious manager Tony Waddington and in a team that included the galloping granddad Stanley Matthews and Peter Dobing. Unlike United, Stoke granted Viollet a testimonial.

His marriage to Barbara, like his truncated United career, also failed to stand the test of time. They had married when Dennis was seventeen and Barbara pregnant with their first son, Roger, who had been named after Roger Byrne.

'Dennis became an outrageous womanizer,' says Doherty. 'I was always having to find alibis for him.'

He developed a particular passion for Jewish girls, admiring their dark looks and their unabashed candour.

And as Albert Scanlon points out irreverently: 'With Dennis's conk, he could have passed for one of them!'

Helen Greeph was sixteen years old and working in her father's Manchester jewellery shop, Brizendens on Deansgate, during her school holidays when she first met Viollet. Her father initially disapproved: 'A nice Jewish girl running off with a footballer? What do you think?' laughs Helen. Viollet was not Jewish and was also eighteen years older, but there was no doubt that Helen made a big impression on the footballer, as she did on a lot of others, notably Albert Scanlon.

'I can remember a year after the crash going to a Jewish Association do at Sale Locarno,' recalls Scanlon. 'There was this girl in charge of the tombola and I remember her swaying through the crowd in an emerald green dress and with no shoes on. Later, her mum and dad asked me to their house and told me to bring a friend, so I took Albert Quixall. Albert fell in love with her mother.'

The attraction between Helen Greeph and Dennis Viollet was mutual.

'I met Dennis when I was sixteen and I used to see him around town after that,' she says. 'Once, in the New Theatre Bar, I was chatting with Dennis and Marlene Shapiro, Bobby Charlton's ex-girlfriend. Marlene was madly in love with Dennis, who carried on just like a single fellow. But I was determined not to be charmed by him. I had a boyfriend at the time and he wouldn't let me meet him. He kept me in the car because he said I would fall for him as all the women did. And it's true, men and women were so attracted to him.

'Dennis was a ladies' man, and not a womanizer and there is a difference. He liked women and he treated them with such respect. Dennis never discussed his conquests, this reputation he got was his French blood – Vee-o-lay don't forget – and he was determined to enjoy every minute of the life that was left to him.

'It was a very difficult situation. Here I was having this affair with Dennis and still living at home. I got a job in Blackpool demonstrating in a department store and Dennis would drive over two or three times a week. My dad was a really rigid disciplinarian and eventually I left home and got a job as a demonstrator, one of the Living Fire Girls. I got a flat, but never saw him for three years. But then he came to America in 1967 to play for Baltimore, I followed him out, went back home, went out again in 1968 and by then he and Barbara had started divorce proceedings.'

They were married in September 1969 and lived at Number Two Cherry Tree Road, in Northern Moor, Wythenshawe, but life after playing proved difficult. Viollet got a job with Preston coaching, played a season for Linfield and then had a disastrous spell with Crewe Alexandra.

'We really struggled then,' says Helen. 'He had to sign on the dole and there seemed to be nothing on the horizon. But then someone phoned and asked if we would go to

America. We came back here in March 1973 and were at Baltimore, Columbia, Maryland and Washington Diplomats. At Boston, Noel Cantwell was in charge and Liptons Tea, who owned the franchise, then moved it to Jacksonville, where Gerry Daly, Peter Simpson and Keith Weller also played. We had wonderful times, had a lot of fun, and then bought a house in Foxborough. This is where he built his wonderful reputation, the community thought the world of him. Dennis always had a great feeling for Jewish people. There was no religion in our life, but if anyone said anything anti-Semitic he would just blow up. He had been to Auschwitz and Belsen.

'He stayed pally with all the boys. Greggy he was very fond of but was always saying: "He's mad, he's wild." He told me this story about Greggy giving Dennis a lift to the ground and on the way they passed Alan Ball Snr waiting in a lay-by for a lift.

'Now Greggy couldn't stand Alan Ball Snr and when Dennis said: "H, there's Alan, aren't you going to stop and pick him up?" Harry said: "Fuck him" and just drove on.'

Harry Gregg recalls the first time he began to worry about Viollet's health. 'It was 1997 and we were due to fly out to Munich for the European Cup Final between Juventus and Borussia Dortmund, this at the invitation of UEFA. They booked me into Manchester Airport before the flight out to Munich next day and that night the hotel room phone rang: "Greggy, it's me Tricky." He came up to my room and there he was. Now Dennis was a man who was immaculate on the field and off it, but he was a mess in an old American-style pullover. He stood there and he said: "You are looking well" and I said: "So are you" and I thought: who's the biggest liar? The way he talked was all funny and he was wanting to buy everyone drinks, with American money.

'The following day we flew BEA to Frankfurt and then Lufthansa from there. Half an hour after we arrived in Frankfurt he just vanished; I went to the tannoy and asked them to put a call out: "Mr Gregg is missing his friend Mr Viollet." They must have thought we were fairies. When I caught up with the rest of the lads at Bayern's old ground I said to them: "There is something desperately wrong with Tricky." Then he got lost at the game and got the wrong flight home to America, by all accounts. When Helen rang up and told us the worst I mentioned the knock he got on his head at Munich and she was screaming: "That's where the tumour was."'

The date on the calendar Viollet dreaded, inevitably, was 6 February, every 6 February. Helen recalls: 'He would say: "Is it 6 February today? He always got a funny feeling on 6 February. He was a very private person but he did open up after a drink and probably if I'm honest I would admit he did drink a little bit too much. Once he started he would consume a fair amount. One particular night he started talking about it. When he became ill, the February after that was the fortieth anniversary and Dennis started to cry: "I'll never see them again, Duncan and Eddie and Roger." What happens with a brain tumour is that your long-term memory becomes very sharp. He never used to cry but he became very emotional when he was ill.

'I don't know what I would have done without that money from the Munich testimonial because he had no insurance – the renewal date was just after he fell ill – and we had used up all our savings on his treatment. You can't go through life feeling bitter about it. Greggy's terrible, he won't let it go; Ray Wood died feeling bitter about Munich.

'The club helped. When he was sick I wrote to them and they sent $10,000, twice. Martin Edwards came to Dennis's memorial service at Old Trafford and was charming. Ken Merritt, the secretary, had always been very helpful. But it was all I had to live on for the rest of my life. Dennis adored America, we laughed all the time, and it was a really fun marriage. I have been very lucky, and I don't think I would have got married if I hadn't met Dennis. I was bowled over by him, luckily it seemed to go the other way, too.

'What he did for the kids in this area. There was one boy called Dylan who had only one arm and Dennis adored him and vice versa. We sold all his medals and memorabilia and raised about $10,000 for it. At the end of January, I thought he had Alzheimers. He started to forget things and he was not like that, he was always very neat and tidy but that went by the board. Once he went to the loo in a local restaurant and couldn't remember his way back to the table. He started feeling dizzy and then saying he could smell a sweet smell. He went away with the team, Team Cyclone, in 1997 and I got a phone call in the middle of the night: "Coach is not well, Mrs Viollet. He thinks he is back in Jacksonville and he kept turning and walking away during our game."'

Helen took him to the doctor, he had a brain scan and it was discovered there were lesions on his brain. Then a biopsy found the tumour. Steroids helped for a time, but 'we knew they had to remove it,' says Helen. 'They got most of the tumour, but we knew it was terminal. He had a bleed to his brain, more surgery to remove clots, which lasted twenty-four hours, but he never walked again.

'There was chemotherapy and radiation and in January and February of 1998 he started to improve and began to walk a bit with help. He got presented with the key to the city of Jacksonville, which was very touching, but then he started to deteriorate and they told me it had spread. Then came the last birthday, in September, the last Thanksgiving, the last Christmas, the last day in St Augustine, and the last three weeks of life.

'In hospital he had a seizure one morning and he was on life support. But there was nothing they could do, so we took him off life support, and got him into a hospice. On the Saturday afternoon, just after three o'clock, Dennis died, listening to Mozart and with Rachel and myself holding his hand. Not a bad way to leave this world when you think about it.'

After Dennis Viollet had gone, 6 February began to take on even more for his widow, too, and on that date a year later she found herself, for reasons she struggles to explain, seated in St Peter's Episcopal Church in Foxborough for a memorial service open to anyone missing loved ones. Two minutes after arrival, a combination of the music, the occasion, the date and time had her sobbing uncontrollably. But . . . 'I dried up as I could hear Den saying, "It's not even begun yet and you're already blubbering!"

'The service took about an hour, then everyone was invited to go down the aisle to the altar, light a candle, state their name and anything specific about the person they had recently lost.

'Suddenly I received a nod from a sweet lady and as I was the only one who had chosen to sit on the left side of the back row, which also happened to be the last row called, I was a little disconcerted to find myself walking last and alone down the aisle towards the altar. I lit the candle that had been given to me and just as I was about to say, "Remembering my beloved husband Dennis Viollet," there came, for no obvious reason, six words of very clear instruction and startling clarity, "Don't forget to mention the lads!"'

So, in a small church in a city a long, long way from Moss Side, Manchester and the great arenas he had graced, a Busby Babe and 'the lads' were remembered.

Viollet's play had been distinguished by his opportunism in front of goal – 179 goals in 294 appearances with another sixty-six in his five seasons with Stoke – and his sharp reflexes. All of these qualities were inherited by his youngest daughter Rachel. Most of Dennis's savings, including the sale of some of his footballing mementoes, went on tennis lessons for the little girl born on 11 February 1972. They were not wasted, and both Dennis and Helen had their reward when Rachel became British number one and appeared at Wimbledon in 1996, losing to eventual winner Martina Hingis in the second round. She retains her British passport and fondly remembers the annual visits to Manchester and her father's guided tours around the theatre in which he fulfilled so many dreams.

The last word should belong to Harry Gregg. As he fiercely points out, he was not a Busby Babe but over the years has become what amounts to their representative on Earth and a sort of niggling conscience for the football club they all once served. On the airfield at Munich, when the hideous crashing and grinding had given way to an eerie silence, the United goalkeeper showed outstanding bravery and at least three people, including his countryman Jackie Blanchflower, undoubtedly owed their lives to the goalkeeper. He found Bert Whalley lying under the fuselage, unmarked and with his eyes wide open, dragged Charlton and Viollet by the seat straps away from the wreckage, and tended to Busby and Blanchflower. Hearing a baby cry he ignored the entreaties of Captain Thain 'to run you silly bugger' and found the child and her mother.

But the hero of Munich, an epithet he hates, also looked down on the bodies of his team-mates, and saw the suffering of their families. The nightmare of the crash has remained with him ever since, although he can claim now: 'I have not one slightest bit of bitterness about the whole damned thing. I had a wife and child I never thought I'd see again and I never even gave the money a thought. Over the years I swear there has been no bitterness, only what I saw as injustice. Some people, forty years later, received a sum of money: the relatives, survivors, through the public shelling out, not the club. Certainly there are times in my life that I have upset people when they have done something I think is unjust. If something comes up I think is wrong I stand up and say it.

'But I've never been a hard man in my life. In some ways I'm actually a coward. Like when the doctor told me Mavis, my first wife, had cancer. I couldn't get out of the hospital quick enough. I couldn't face her and didn't know what to say. It was only when I saw her up at the window smiling at me that I went back. And she comforted me; I didn't comfort her. Martin Edwards said Munich was nothing to do with him; at least he was up front about it. Others have tried to live on the fact they were Babes and they were not. It has become an industry to certain individuals. But I have no bitterness. If I offered you £100 million, would it buy you the life I have had? I have memories you could never buy.'

When I last saw him, Harry Gregg was framed by the hall light in the doorway of his home, peering a farewell into a stormy Antrim night: Don Quixote in an Irish Football Association tracksuit.

EPILOGUE

Conway Close was, and probably still is for all I know, a large figure of eight of semi-detached homes surrounding two grassy circles in Alkrington, a large residential area in the north Manchester suburb of Middleton. From 1954 to 1959, my parents paid Middleton Town Council twenty-five shillings a week for the two-and-a-half bedrooms, kitchen, lounge and large garden which constituted Number 41, fronting the smaller of the two greens on what we knew as the Bottom End. The move to Alkrington represented a sort of urban promotion from the previous family home in Browning Road, Boarshaw, a charmless estate down the hill on the other side of Oldham Road, where the chemicals from the local dye factory had had an alarming effect on the sensitive skin of my younger brother. That, and the credit points earned by my parents from their war service – Dad in the Parachute Regiment and Mum in the Women's Auxiliary

Air Force – earned us what we perceived, in every possible way, as a move in an upward direction.

Alkrington, later to market itself successfully as Alkrington Garden Village, was the posh end of Middleton and the surrounding streets were lined by the large detached houses of north Manchester's *nouveau riche* none too pleased, it must be said, to see a council estate appear almost overnight in their midst. Conway Close was looked on by this collection of minor company directors, scrap-metal merchants and shop owners, described scornfully by my mother as 'folk who think they are something they are not', as a plebeian redoubt, an impression reinforced by the fact that as its name suggests there was only one road into the Close and the same road out. In fact, it was a homely little world where every family knew next door's business, and a community that was fairly typical of post-war Manchester with a discernible sense of optimism informing what was basically a working-class existence. Even now, after fifty years, I can recall the faces and occupations of most of the adults on the Close, along with the names of their children. I say optimism, because even for children born too late to remember the war there was a sense of emerging from a dark tunnel into daylight. Rationing had ended, there was a new queen on the throne, Everest had been climbed, Bannister had run his four-minute mile and the first satellite was soon to be launched into orbit. Nearer home, on Conway Close, three or four families owned

black-and-white televisions, motor cars and had the where-
withal to send children to grammar school. Some, or so it
was whispered, spent their summer holidays in Cleveleys
or Southport, rather than that Mecca of the works outing,
Blackpool.

And then there was sport.

After the war the recreation-hungry crowds, starved of
professional competition for so long, flooded back to
Manchester's arenas. The other Old Trafford, down at the
southern end of Warwick Road, was home to Lancashire
Cricket Club where an ancient bell summoned thousands
to the opening of play. Surrey were the acknowledged
masters in those days, but Lancashire ran them close and
although there was a touch of northern parochialism when
we attempted to claim their Yorkshire-born spinner as
almost one of our own, no one could ever forget the Ashes
summer of 1956, and the sight of Jim Laker, white sweater
draped casually over his shoulder, sauntering off the worn
turf having taken nineteen Australian wickets. The city
centre had its own Ice Palace close by Strangeways prison
and many a small fortune could be won, or more usually
lost, at Manchester racecourse out by Broughton Park.
Belle Vue, the Disneyland of the North of England and a
wonderfully vulgar magic kingdom of animals, fearsome
switchback rides, an exotic and peerless speedway team
and even a Wall of Death, was situated on Hyde Road in
West Gorton and easily accessible by bus or tram from the

city centre. The park was also capacious enough to host the All England Athletics Championships as well as brass band contests, flower shows, fabulous fireworks displays and Mothers' Union rallies. Close by, the smoke-filled and atmospheric King's Hall staged world-class boxing contests and equally popular wrestling shows, usually featuring the local heroes/villains, the Pye Brothers. For those children unable to afford a ride on the hair-raising Belle Vue Bobs, or even Annie the elephant, there was always north Manchester's vast green playground, Heaton Park, where boys in underpants and girls with skirts tucked into knickers splashed in the sandpits and paddling pools, unchaperoned, unabashed, and unaware that these seemingly endless summers could not last for ever.

For most, however, and certainly for my parents, the burgeoning affluence of the early Fifties, the sense that the future did hold a golden promise, found its physical form in the Busby Babes and their youthful, exuberant omnipotence. The nine- and ten-year-olds on Conway Close may not have put it quite that way, but we certainly aspired to something close to those qualities.

The larger green at the top end of the Close was used mainly by walkers of family pets too idle to venture into the open countryside that still surrounded Alkrington in those days and this, combined with its domed surface, made it unsuitable for ball games. The bottom end, the size of one half of a football field, was flat and verdant and for four years saw some of Manchester United's finest moments pre-played, or occasionally replayed, depending on the result. Middleton, and north Manchester as a whole, was not typical United territory as even in the first successful days of the Babes there was a parochialism about the game; most people tended to support their nearest football side, in our cases Rochdale or Oldham. The maximum wage ensured that these clubs, and others in Lancashire like Bolton, Preston, Blackpool and Burnley, retained their best players, most of whom were local, too. Preston had Finney for the whole of his illustrious career, Bolton kept Lofthouse and Blackpool a whole host of luminaries, notably Matthews and Mortensen. My grandfather on my mother's side supported Rochdale all his life and one Saturday persuaded me to visit Spotland, where the crowd watched in almost total silence. In the absence of a stadium clock Pa would check the minutes remaining from a gold watch, attached to his waistcoat by a long, silver chain, the material rewards for his fifty years' service with Robert Cawley and Sons, dyeworkers, of Bowker Bank, Crumpsall.

Most football fealties, like favourite family artefacts, were invariably handed down from father to son – if my Dad had been a Bury supporter I would undoubtedly forever more be extolling the virtues of the giants of Gigg Lane – but fate had placed four regular United fan-fathers and a commensurate number of sons on Conway Close.

On match days there, we were the Busby Babes; the opposition came from the surrounding streets and were basically anonymous cannon fodder for a team that could field the juvenile alter egos of Duncan Edwards at wing-half, Dennis Viollet as the lone striker, Eddie Colman as the Edwards/Viollet link and Ray Wood (later Harry Gregg) in goal. Edwards was always impersonated by Malcolm Watson, mainly by dint of his size. His father was the chief attendant at Middleton Baths and Malcolm himself was given to puffing out his chest and leaping high in the air to head an imaginary ball before a game. Peter Ramsbottom, the smallest and spottiest of us by a long way, took the role of Eddie Colman with a passable imitation of the swivelling hips. I coveted the predatory, skinny swagger of Dennis Viollet and had even, at the age of eleven, experimented with Brylcreem.

The arrival of Gregg at Old Trafford early in 1957 had been signalled by an almost total metamorphosis in Stuart Hebden, who when not keeping goal was the full-time Alkrington hoodlum, the type of boy who sat on the back seat of buses, features already defined at the age of ten by a mixture of cunning and guilt. Stuart was always either causing trouble or contemplating it.

On the Close, he had once been, like Wood, an adherent to positional play; now he was Crazy Harry. Pre-Gregg he had never strayed from the imaginary white line defined by a pile of school blazers and a large concrete lamp-post, but now spent as much time out of goal as in. His aggressive nature was also satisfied by lunatic charges into attacker and defender alike, the justification for this being the day he had seen Gregg, in one of his early matches for United, wipe out an opposing centre-forward, and the startled Edwards, in one clattering assault. He also took to wearing his father's cloth cap which flopped ludicrously over his ears along with a green woollen jersey, also several sizes too big.

Behind Hebden and his goal a mongrel bitch we called Peggy performed, without ever being asked or ordered, the roles of backstop and ball girl. No one knew where she came from or even if Peggy was her real name, but for three years, summer and winter she would appear at the same time every day, around 3.30 pm, almost as if she had heard the school bell. In summer, as with so many goal-keepers, she converted seamlessly to wicket-keeper, leaping, diving and catching behind the lamp-post which now represented three cricket stumps and a set of bails. Once the slavering enthusiast managed to stump a startled batsman who strayed from his crease by rolling the ball slowly from mouth on to wicket,

When we were not pretending to be the Busby Babes we were watching the real thing and Saturdays – every Saturday for if the first-team were away we simply joined up to 20,000 others to watch the reserves – were spent saucer-eyed with foolish gratitude on the Popular Side at

Old Trafford. The preparations for the pilgrimage were marked at number 41 by a ritual akin to slipping into a favourite pair of shoes and would begin precisely at 12.30 pm with the red-and-white barred scarf and woolly coat, gloves and bonnet. My father would load the flask of Bovril, the abiding beverage of football Saturdays, and I would be awarded custody of the bar of dairy milk chocolate. Finally, with the smile of a conjuror pulling a rabbit out of his hat, Dad would unearth the box from its hiding place under the stairs.

The box had probably once held fruit, but was now employed as a wobbly, wooden plinth from which I could peer over adult heads in the Old Trafford stand. It was also as useful a gauge of the swift march of adolescence as a set of scales and a tape measure. When I had first gone to see the Busby Babes in 1955, playing, as I recall, in an FA Youth Cup semi-final, it was stood on its end with Dad's grip on my shoulders ensuring that I stayed there, unmoved by the human eddies of the surrounding terraces. Three years later the box could be placed more securely on its side and had acquired some extra wooden slats by way of reinforcement.

The weekly journey to Old Trafford followed a time-honoured and never varying course: a ten-minute walk from Conway Close to Manchester New Road, the 63 bus through Blackley and Harpurhey to Cannon Street in the city centre, a swift march up Cross Street to Albert Square and its sooty Town Hall and on to Central railway station where a short, rattling ride took us to the Old Trafford halt close by the ground.

There, the doors were flung open and, like bathwater released by a plug, the train's contents spilled out on to the platform to join an even larger throng heading towards the ground, a huge multi-legged insect, uncoordinated and yet controlled. On my first trip to Old Trafford I had been borne away by the swell and was only tearfully reunited with dad and the box some ten minutes later, thanks to a rescue operation performed by three grizzled male fans, one of whom shepherded me to dry land by the station pickets while the others went in search of my anxious father.

Our favoured viewpoint lay low down on what was known as the Popular Side, now the North Stand, but since you had to queue for tickets and the stewards simply closed the turnstiles when one stand was full we also spent time in the Stretford End and even in the Scoreboard End. This could be a disconcerting place to watch a football match for at approximately 3.45 pm all eyes in the other three stands would turn in that direction to catch the half-time scores that appeared, at interminable intervals and at the bidding of some hidden hand, opposite the letters running from A–Z in the huge wooden structure. For young supporters in that section it was like being thrust suddenly on to a massive stage.

There were other fathers, other sons. Some children would perch on the terrace crush rails, their places there enforced by what amounted to unwritten, and unchallenged, squatters' rights and one regular little group of father, two sons and daughter, travelled most Saturdays from Leeds. The girl carried a red-and-white rattle almost as big as herself and we regarded all four with a mixture of curiosity and awe, baffled by the fortitude, stamina and financial resources that had carried them all the way from the other end of the known world.

Around us in the stand, stools borrowed from family living-rooms performed a similar function to that of my box. One father and son bore a lovingly constructed three-part prefabricated pulpit which slotted neatly together like a Lego set and even contained a slot for two size-four feet on the top. Individual sections, explained the proud owner, could be discarded as the boy grew and the deliberate, studied care that had gone into this in some suburban workshop could only be marvelled at. This was an eccentric little club the exclusivity of which was signalled by the bashful, nodding smiles and shrugs of resignation among the fathers I was later to associate with Volkswagen Beetle drivers.

The memories of Old Trafford of those days are, the occasional defeat apart, of happy wonder; a Spielbergian fantasy of small boys straying into a big boys' world, of swaying masses swilling around us on the vast, open terraces, the cheerful camaraderie of the supporters, Johnny Ray and Jimmy Young on the echoing tannoy. Once the man in charge of the turntable forgot himself and put on Guy Mitchell and *Singing the Blues*, until the crowd gaily reminded him we were the red end of Manchester. Even the Old Trafford smog which, combined with Manchester's traditional greyness, turned day into night and hung a post-apocalyptic gloom over the place, held a unique charm. Smoke from the waiting steam trains billowed in huge clouds over the south stand to occasionally obscure the score box and the exhalations of a thousand Woodbines and Hamlets rose to mingle with the airborne miasma from the factories, foundries and engineering works of nearby Trafford Park. All this may partly explain why all the flickering recollections of that era are framed in monochrome; that and the fact that every opposing team seemed to be clad in varying unglamorous mixtures of black and white – Preston, Bolton, Tottenham, Newcastle and even Real Madrid. After late October, too, there was little or no greenery left on the playing surface and while love for a particular football side is invariably blind, I can say, quite truthfully, that the only colours I can recall from Old Trafford of those days are the red jerseys of the home side.

In April 1957, Real Madrid arrived for the first time, to grace United's first genuine home tie in the European Cup and the first played under Old Trafford's new floodlights. Nothing, before or since, has ever come close to matching the spellbinding wonder of those first nights in Europe, the aching romance of each occasion made even more poignant now by the fact that they were to be, for me at least, so fleeting. The hours after dark are always an adventure for a small boy, but to make the long journey to Old Trafford into a night which held both smiling promise and fearful anticipation was to be the elemental experience of childhood. The beckoning lights in the distance, which could be spotted from a mile away by children bold enough to worm a way to the right side of the railway carriage through overcoats reeking of machine oil and cigarette smoke, resembled a magic kingdom in the sky assembled by Disney. That first sighting of foreigners on Old Trafford and the exotica of their names added even more glamour to the occasion. On Saturdays we had booed and hissed the likes of Clamp and Flowers of Wolves, Lofthouse of Bolton and, particularly, McParland of Aston Villa. Now we simply gawped at the likes of Gento, Kopa, Munoz and Di Stefano; they may as well have come from another planet. Nights like these, or so I thought, would last forever.

Thirteen days after Munich, we embarked on my father's last journey to Old Trafford. It was a confusing but, in its own way, delineating night for while I knew that I would never see the Busby Babes again the concepts of tragedy are lost on an adolescent mind. While I certainly knew the emotions of greed, joy, fear, love and loathing, sentiment is the province of the mature. For a child of twelve the early twenties represent middle age and for grown-ups, even grown-ups called Babes, to die seemed perfectly natural. But I did understand the source of my father's tears that night.

The spaces for the names of the home team in the programme were symbolically blank, but even had Murphy been able to name a side in time for the printers their identity would have remained just as much of a mystery; there were strangers in the jerseys of our heroes.

Three other memories of that night: the roar which greeted the announcement of the first United name, that of Gregg, and an equal clamour – even though Bill had never been one of our favourites – which greeted the second, Foulkes. There were screams of grief mixed with exhortation from the massed bunch of women in head scarves bordering the players' tunnel, as always their large plastic handbags draped on the white picket fencing in front of them, and an adult voice some ten rows behind us, bawling every thirty seconds or so throughout the whole of the ninety minutes '*Dun-can, Dun-can*', as if enough repetitions of the name would raise the young prince from his death bed. Sheffield Wednesday, the palled opposition that night, didn't have an earthly.

The strength of dynasties – and Manchester United surely rival the Kennedys in the extent of their glamour and the breadth of their tragedy – is that there is always someone left to pick up the banner from the fallen. Murphy performed superhuman feats of recruitment, motivation and organization and with a wind of worldwide sympathy and emotion behind them his team of raw reserves and imported has-beens staggered on to Wembley. By then, Manchester United had ceased to be just another football club.

Back on the Close, the Alkrington Babes died, too. The names of Pearson or Crowther didn't have the same resonance as Edwards or Colman and gradually the games fizzled out. We lost our backstop when she was run over by a decorator's van in nearby Mount Road, the whereabouts of her real home and the identity of her owners remaining a mystery to the end. My fruit-box pedestal was relegated to the outside shed where it was used to store firelighters, a small axe and a coal scoop and there were other subtle shifts in our lives. Colour television, the swinging Sixties, soccer hooliganism and George Best were just round the corner. Secondary school, alcohol, cigarettes, girls, marriage, divorce and all those days of squandered youth and hopeless optimism lay ahead.

It was only later, much later, that I began to understand the essence of the Lost Babes; that their purity, innocence and beauty mirrored something irretrievable within us all. It's the reason Joy Byrne christened her son Roger, John Doherty his eldest boy Mark and Jimmy Armfield chose the name Duncan for his son. It is the fundamental that will bind forever Harry Gregg of County Antrim, Rajko Mitic of Belgrade, Rino Gambone of Bilston, the lady (and surely it must be a lady) from Doncaster who places a red flower on David Pegg's grave every week and the anonymous mourners who gather outside Old Trafford every 6 February.

Dad, of course, had recognized this at once, for he never went back after 19 February and when, two days later, Duncan Edwards lost his parabolic fight for life it confirmed what he had suspected: that something true, decent and valorous had been extinguished forever.

Unlike his eldest son, almost forty-five years later, he never made the mistake of going back to hunt for ghosts and he bade farewell to Old Trafford and Manchester United with what I now recognize as an awful prescience.

'Things,' said my father, who was not very old but was certainly very wise, 'will never be the same again.'

INDEX